RESEARCHING
YOUR
JAMAICAN
FAMILY

Researching Your Jamaican Family

Jennifer O'Sullivan-Sirjue
with
Pansy Robinson

Arawak publications
17 Kensington Crescent   Apt 5
Kingston 5   Jamaica

© 2007 by Jennifer O'Sullivan-Sirjue with Pansy Robinson
All rights reserved. Published 2007
ISBN 976 8189 48 6

11 10 9 8 7
e d c b a

NATIONAL LIBRARY OF JAMAICA CATALOGUING IN PUBLICATION DATA
O'Sullivan-Sirjue, Jennifer
　　Researching your Jamaican family / Jennifer O'Sullivan-Sirjue with Pansy Robinson

　　　　p. : ill., maps ;   cm.

　　Bibliography : p.　　. – Includes index

　　ISBN 976-8189-48-6 (pbk)

　　1. Family – Jamaica - History.   2. Family – Jamaica - Research.   3. Genealogy
　　4. Jamaica – Genealogy – Handbooks, manuals, etc.   5. Jamaica – Social conditions
　　I. Robinson, Pansy   II. Title

　　929.2　　dc 22

Cover design by David McLeod
Book design by Annika Lewinson-Morgan

Set in 10.5/11.75pt Cantoria MT with President BT

Contents

- List of figures, maps, tables *vii*
- Acknowledgements *ix*
- Introduction *1*

CHAPTER 1 • RESEARCHING YOUR FAMILY HISTORY *4*
    1.1 Why a family history? *4*
    1.2 Getting started *5*
    1.3 Information you will need *6*
    1.4 Oral sources *8*
    1.5 Drawing the family tree *9*
    1.6 Sharing the information *12*
    1.7 Other reunions and get-togethers *15*

CHAPTER 2 • COMPILING YOUR FAMILY HISTORY *17*
    2.1 Further research *17*
    2.2 Local sources – Written *18*
    2.3 Local sources – Audio-visual *37*
    2.4 Local places to obtain information *38*
    2.5 Overseas sources *51*

CHAPTER 3 • ETHNIC ROOTS OF JAMAICAN FAMILIES *53*
    3.1 Ethnic groups who came *55*
    3.2 Composition of Jamaica's population *72*
    3.3 Place names as clues to ethnicity *74*
    3.4 Family names as clues to ethnicity *76*
    3.5 Family life in Jamaica *78*

CHAPTER 4 • JAMAICAN HISTORY AND YOUR FAMILY *83*
    4.1 Communication *85*
    4.2 Defence, law and order *88*
    4.3 Education and culture *91*
    4.4 Freedom and civil rights *96*
    4.5 Government *101*
    4.6 Land ownership and inheritance *103*
    4.7 Migration patterns *104*

4.8 Money *110*
4.9 Natural hazards *112*
4.10 Religion *113*

CHAPER 5 ♦ FAMILY DATA FOR FUTURE GENERATIONS *118*

♦ Appendix: Maps *120*

♦ Select Bibliography *122*

♦ Index *124*

Figures
Fig. 1.1 Basic information to obtain about each family member *7*
Fig. 1.2 Examples of various kinds of family tree *10*

Maps
1. Jamaica – Main population centres *x*
2. Lands of origin of Jamaicans *54*
3. Maroon settlements and some free villages in Jamaica *64*
4. Location of some of the estates employing Indian immigrants 1879-1921 *68*

Appendix: Maps
A. Jamaica – parish boundaries: 1664 *120*
B. Jamaica – parish boundaries: 1738 *120*
C. Jamaica – parish boundaries: 1844 *121*
D. Jamaica: 1867 to present – county and parish boundaries *121*

Tables
2.1 Some Christian denominations, year established and Jamaican head offices *25*
2.2 Jamaican parishes, 1664 to the present *26*
2.3 Information on birth, marriage and death certificates *39*
2.4 A sample of newspapers offered by towns *43*
3.1 Arrival dates of some early European settlers *56*
3.2 Increase in number of lots under 10 acres, 1840-1865 *60*
3.3 Location and origin of some free villages *61*
3.4 Some areas of settlement of voluntary indentured Africans *65*
3.5 Jamaica's population by native country, Census 1861 *73*
3.6 Ethnic origin of Jamaica's population: 1982, 1991 and 2001 *74*
3.7 Ethnic origin of some Jamaican place names *75*
3.8 Ethnic origin of some Jamaican surnames *77*
4.1 Pre-emancipation Free schools *92*
4.2 Some secondary schools established after Emancipation *93*
4.3 Earliest free villages *99*
4.4 Different forms of government under English rule, 1655-1962 *101*
4.5 Some pre-emancipation German immigration *105*
4.6 Distribution of population by ethnic groups, 1690-1830 *107*
4.7 Indentured workers from Africa, 1840-1865 *108*
4.8 Dates of arrival of Chinese indentured workers, 1854-1888 *108*
4.9 Indentured workers from India, 1845-1914 *108*

NOTE: Relevant references are conveniently located throughout the text

Acknowledgments

Researching Your Jamaican Family is a tribute to my family members, who over these twenty-odd years have journeyed with me in doing our family trees (both maternal and paternal sides). The enthusiasm and good times shared have contributed much to our family life.

My parents Linda O'Sullivan neé Purkiss and Leslie (Bill) O'Sullivan always informed us about our relationship to different family members. Our lives were filled with paying visits to family and in turn having family members, foreign and local, visit and stay over. However, it is to my cousin Carl Pearce, resident in Canada, that I give credit, for opening my eyes to the value of a family tree.

To my friend Pansy Robinson I owe deep gratitude. Our reacquaintance after the passage of time, along with a shared interest in family genealogy and family history greatly facilitated the completion of this work.

I am indebted also to friends and relatives who critiqued draft stages of this text: Barbara Williams, Darcy Wright, Pansy and Hernal Hamilton, Jacinth Taylor, Marlene and Maurice Dilworth, Sashenee Duval, Omari Dilworth, and Jane and Roy Dodman.

Last, but not least, I must put on record the support, interest and information given to me by my husband, Wilbert Sirjue.

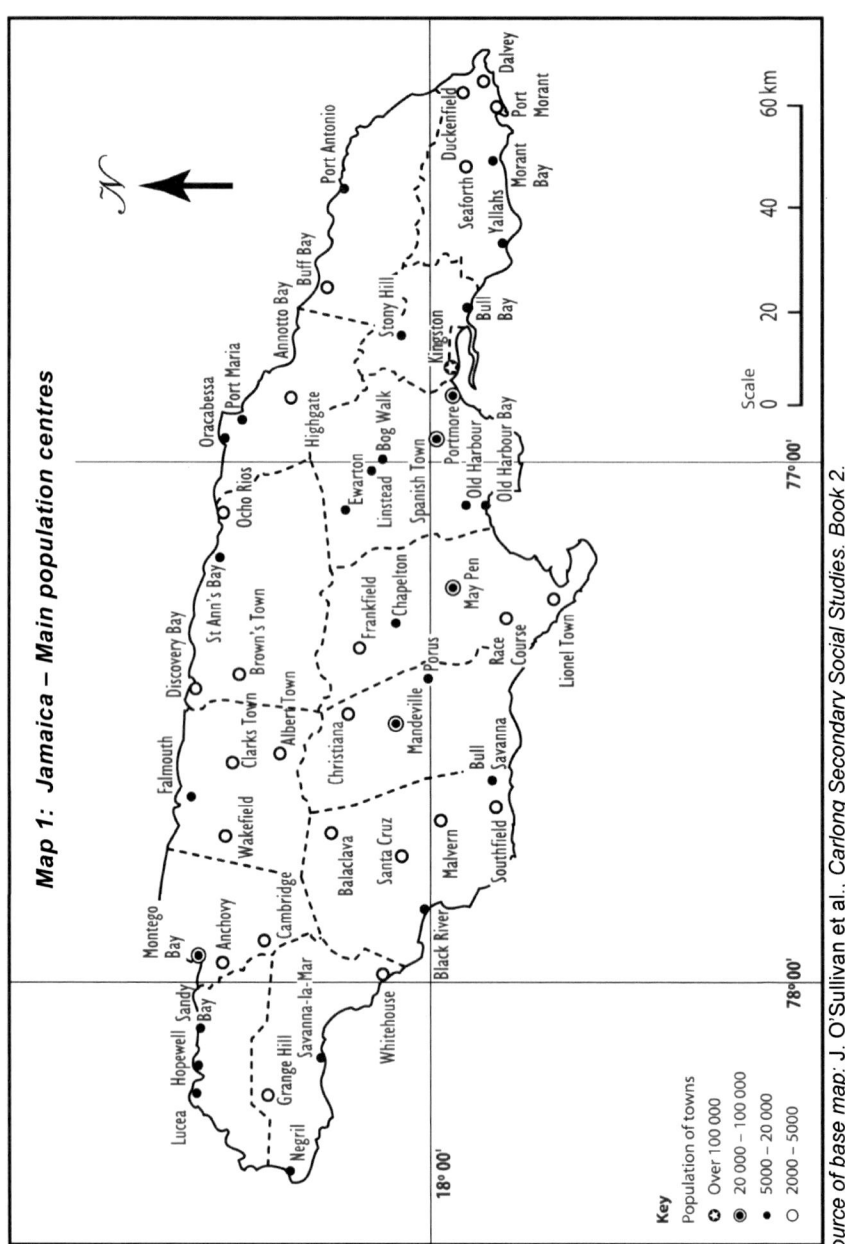

Map 1: Jamaica – Main population centres

Source of base map: J. O'Sullivan et al., Carlong Secondary Social Studies. Book 2. Jamaica: Land and People. Carlong Publishers.1998: p.110

Introduction

Have you ever wondered how you are related to a cousin or wondered if you are related to persons with your surname? Would you like to satisfy your curiosity about how your great-grand-parents came to live in Jamaica or about relatives who went to live in Panama?

Would you like to collate all the bits and pieces of your family story, fill in the gaps and create a family history package? If you think you know nothing about your family history, you may be surprised to find out how easy it is to get started.

Researching Your Jamaican Family seeks to encourage individuals and families to indulge in the exciting journey of collecting and sharing family history. This book provides:

- sources of family information
- information on the main ethnic groups in Jamaica
- historical notes on matters that impact family life
- ideas for the ongoing collection of family history for future generations.

Each family is special. So is yours. Don't just read of others and their families. Record your family story – the accomplishments and challenges. Document your family stories in words, sound and pictures. Leave a legacy for your children, nieces, nephews and grandchildren. Contribute to the ongoing process of building your family identity. Get as many family members as possible involved.

Who is a Jamaican?

A Jamaican is
- a person born and living in Jamaica and a person who, prior to 1962, was designated a 'citizen of the United Kingdom and colonies'
- a person born in Jamaica of foreign parents
- a person born overseas of one or two Jamaican parents

Persons who can apply to become Jamaican citizens:
- a person born in another country who after years of being resident in the island applies for and is granted naturalized citizenship
- any man or woman married to a Jamaican

The term 'family' in Jamaica

The term *family* in Jamaica has a wide and inclusive meaning. The nuclear family consisting of mother, father and children is recognized, but so too is the extended family whether or not they live in the same household. The extended family in a household may include all or some of the following relatives – mother, father, siblings, aunts, uncles, cousins, grandparents. The extended family outside the nuclear or extended households consists of other relatives and step relations (half brothers and half sisters).

Jamaicans also use the term *family* to refer to close family friends who care, love and often assume responsibilities 'just as family would'.

Some family traditions

In some families, respect for older family members is shown by use of prefixes. Younger siblings are instructed to address older siblings with the prefix 'Sister' or 'Brother'. 'Cousin' is often used to prefix the names of older cousins, so there is Cousin Nkosi just as there is Sister Beryl, Brother Byron, Uncle Tom, Aunt Luc, Grandpa Bill and Grandma Tiny.

Often younger children are instructed to call an older cousin 'Aunt' or 'Uncle' as a mark of respect. The tradition of also having children call close family friends 'Aunt' and 'Uncle' sometimes results in children and even adults wondering how they are related to an 'Aunt' or 'Uncle'. This is a factor to be aware of and investigate when compiling a family tree.

One other piece of evidence of Jamaicans' concern with family is the listing of family members in death announcements and the additional practice of giving the numbers of sisters, brothers, children, grandchildren and great-grand children of the deceased.

'Going home'

A strong sense of family leads many city folk to visit rural family homes on weekends and holidays. Where family homes are in rural districts, the term 'going to the country' is often repeated with near reverence.

Children are often sent to spend holidays with family members, especially grandparents. Persons from rural communities combine business and pleasure trips with visits to families living in urban areas.

Over the years, tens of thousands of Jamaicans have migrated to different countries. The majority continue the tradition of 'going home'. Christmas, Easter, Emancipation and Independence holidays and are prime visiting periods. Weddings, christenings, birthdays, other anniversaries, family reunions, funerals with the attendant 'set up' (wake) and 'nine-night' are all attended by a steady stream of relatives. Lately, community, school and parish reunions are opening additional opportunities for family gatherings.

Jamaicans who live in Jamaica also delight in visiting relatives overseas. Some family members may even be offended if other members of the family travel to the United States of America or England and choose to stay at a hotel or elsewhere, rather than with relatives.

Researching Your Family History

1.1 Why a Family History?

Researching your family history will be a delightful adventure of discovery of yourself and your ancestors. This alone is a good reason to undertake the work. But there are others. Here, for example, are two Jamaican proverbs that support the wisdom of this effort:

Family stick wi bend but it won't bruk.
(Families may disagree but the family bonds will not be broken)

The farthest of blood is nearer than stranger.
(The bond between extended family is closer than that of friends and acquaintances)

To maintain a 'sense of family', we need to know our family members. We nurture our family relationships by keeping in touch with them. If we don't, we will lose them and an important part of ourselves.

Another good reason to revitalize and maintain our family contact is to allow the younger generation to have a 'sense of family', as well as a sense of belonging to a community, a nation, and a larger world. There is a special need for this today as more Jamaicans emigrate and either become citizens of their new countries of abode or hold dual citizenship. Family ties provide stability during the transition process from country of origin to country of adoption.

A good way to begin to identify family members is to create a family tree showing members of your immediate family and members of each generation as far back as you can go.

1.2 Getting Started

You must begin with some very basic decision making. You must decide whether you want:
- family tree
- family tree and family history
- history only

Whether you are going to research the ancestry of:
- both parents
- one parent only
- one parent at a time

In either case, a further decision must be:
- what information you will collect
- how you will record and store the information
- how you will actually draw the tree and/or record the history
- how you will share the information with other family members

A note of caution

While some family members may not support the idea of tracing your ancestry, others may be proud and impressed by your interest and will go to any means possible to help you find information. Attempt to have as many as possible cooperate with the process by explaining:
- why you want to do this
- how you will do the research
- what you intend to do with the information collected

Who will do the work

Family research requires a lot of patience, time and perseverance. You can choose any of these three options or ways of doing it:

1. You may do it on your own. If you are lucky, you may find that other family members have collected bits of information over the years. Your job will be to collect the material, perhaps add to it and share it in an interesting way.

2. You could divide up the research by giving each family member a specific task. One could, for example, do research from different sources in Jamaica or in other countries. Make sure that each one works back from the known to the unknown.
3. You may contract someone or an institution to do the research. For this you will have to supply some basic information. You could decide to use their services for one or more particular aspects of your research. In either case make sure you have a written agreement about what you want and what the cost is likely to be. Bear in mind that researching family history requires many hours of work and that not all searches achieve positive results. Most institutions, therefore, charge for time spent doing the research.

1.3 Information You Will Need

Your initial research objective will be to compile information about your relatives: your parents, your brothers, sisters, aunts, uncles, cousins, grandparents. What is the kind of information we should be gathering and compiling about each family member? This information is very basic and very personal. You will be compiling information, for example, on each family member's full name; gender; nationality; ethnicity.

A checklist of this basic information would look like Figure 1.1.

As you progress and gather more information, you will probably want to add more questions in order to follow up topics of particular interest. In the category "marriage", for example, you may include the name of the person your family member marries and information about that person's family.

You are dealing with important and sometimes very private issues here, so please note:

1. A family member may not wish to answer all your questions. You need to respect that person's decision.
2. Ask permission if you wish to record the conversation or to take a picture of the person being interviewed.
3. Not all individuals will want to give information about their date of birth, so be tactful.

*Researching
Your Family History*

Figure 1.1 Basic information to obtain about each family member

- Full name: Trevor Page
- Name of parents: Trevor and Linda Page
- Gender: Male
- Ethnicity: Mixed
- Nationality: Jamaican
- Date and place of birth: 10 April 1913
- Date of arrival in Jamaica: Not applicable
- Date of emigration from Jamaica: N/A
- Place(s) of residence: Dias, Hanover
- Occupation(s): Farmer
- Name of spouse: Dorcas Smith
- Date and place of marriage: 10 January 1938
- Name(s) of child(ren): Karen and Carson
- Date and place of divorce: N/A
- Date and place of death: 10 May 1967, Lucea Hospital

Source(s) of data:_____

_____ Date obtained:_____

Other possible sources:_____

1.4 Oral Sources

Your oral sources are family members, family friends and acquaintances in the community (church, workplace, clubs).

Start by talking to your relatives individually and privately – face-to-face, by telephone or by e-mail. Be sure to record all information either on tape or in writing.

Ask individuals to spell their names and the names of all places where they or other family members are living or have lived. As you do your research, look out for variations in spelling of all names – both Christian/ first names, surname/last names and names of places.

For example, early birth records spelt 'Purkis' and later ones show 'Purkiss' for the same family in the same registration district.

Surnames/last names (family names) guide the development of family trees. You will find it easier to track the Surnames/last names of male relatives since married females change their Surnames/last names. In a few cases some married women retain their maiden/family names, adding their husband's Surnames/last names e.g. O'Sullivan-Sirjue. Remember too that there are cases where a child is given its mother's Surname/last name.

You may find differences in the first names by which you know individuals. This is because people use pet names such as 'Precious' (a form of endearment), nick-names such as 'Shortie' (which describes the person), and short forms of names such as Dot for Dorothy.

Find out all you can from older relatives, as they are the ones with information about past family history. Many delight in recalling stories about their younger days and about life in the communities where they lived. You may also find that oral history told by community elders include mention of your family. Jamaica has a strong oral tradition and a lot of the island's folkways and history have been passed down by word of mouth. This is especially true of matters concerning non-whites. The information will also be useful in compiling the family history.

Cross-checking information

Sometimes, people make mistakes about dates and places. You should therefore cross-check information, but without offending the informer. Asking other people about the same event/

information will help you to do this. Tactful questions will also enable you to cross-check information.

Some facts may be better verified by using recorded data which family members may have. These are:

- birth certificates
- christening/baptismal certificates
- marriage certificates
- death certificates

Orders of services from funerals will also serve to confirm dates of birth and death and places of burials.

If you need additional information about births, marriages, deaths, it is useful to research official records (see pages 24-29). When seeking birth records, if there are no registration centres for the district where a family member was born, a larger district, village or town nearby may be the place of registration. Hospitals are also centres for registration of births and deaths. School attendance records may also be helpful in fixing birth dates.

Note that death certificates do not carry dates of birth. In some cases the age shown may have been estimated or rounded off to the nearest year.

1.5 Drawing the Family Tree

Once you have information on names, dates of birth, marriages, death of family members (parents, grandparents, great-grand parents, children, step-parents, step-children, half-brothers, half-sisters, adopted children), you are ready to draw your family tree. One possible tree is shown on page 10. You can adapt it to your needs or design one of your own. I recommend preparing the first sketch of your family tree in pencil as it allows you to make changes easily.

When you have completed your family tree you may wish to develop a complete package to include all or some of the following:

- a copy of your family tree
- a photo album with captions for each photo
- a short story about your family
- short biographies of family members

Researching Your Jamaican Family

Figure 1.2: Examples of various kinds of family tree
 (i) Vertical layout showing family members in descending order starting with oldest members at the top

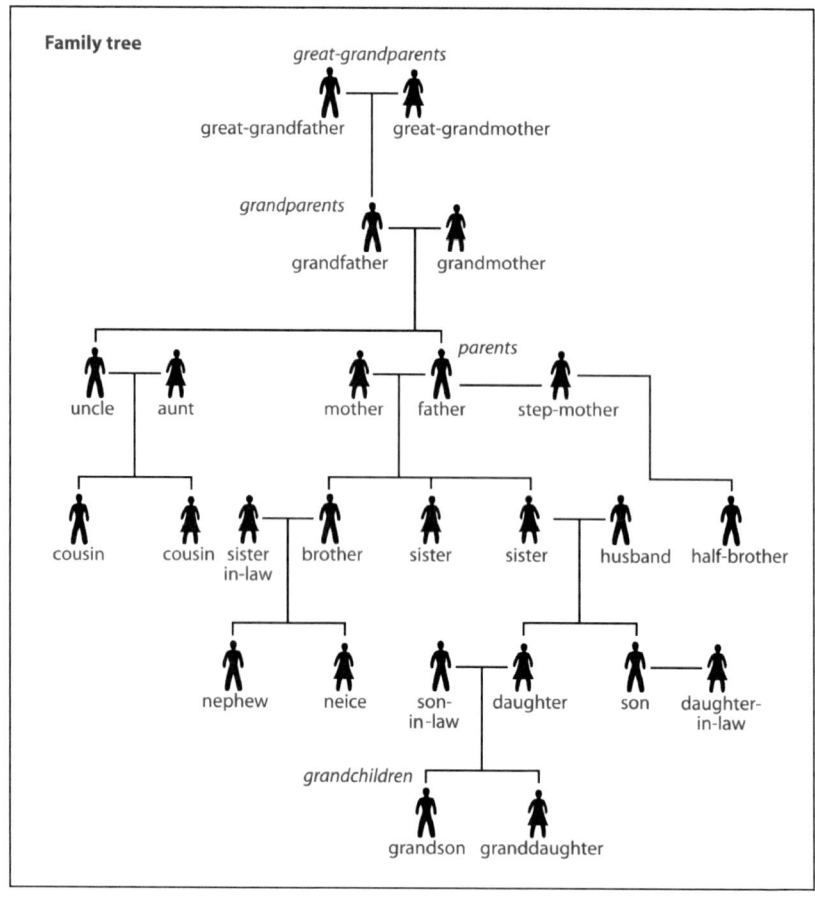

*Researching
Your Family History*

(ii) Horizontal layout starting with oldest members on the left

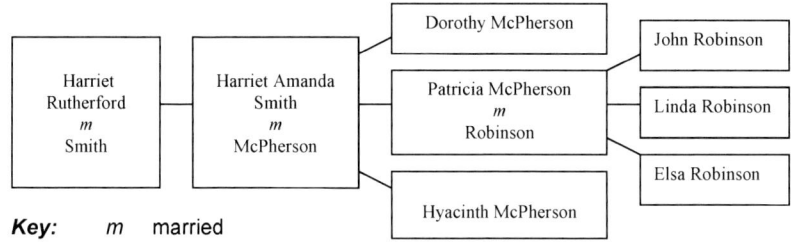

Key: *m*   married

(iii) Vertical layout complete with names

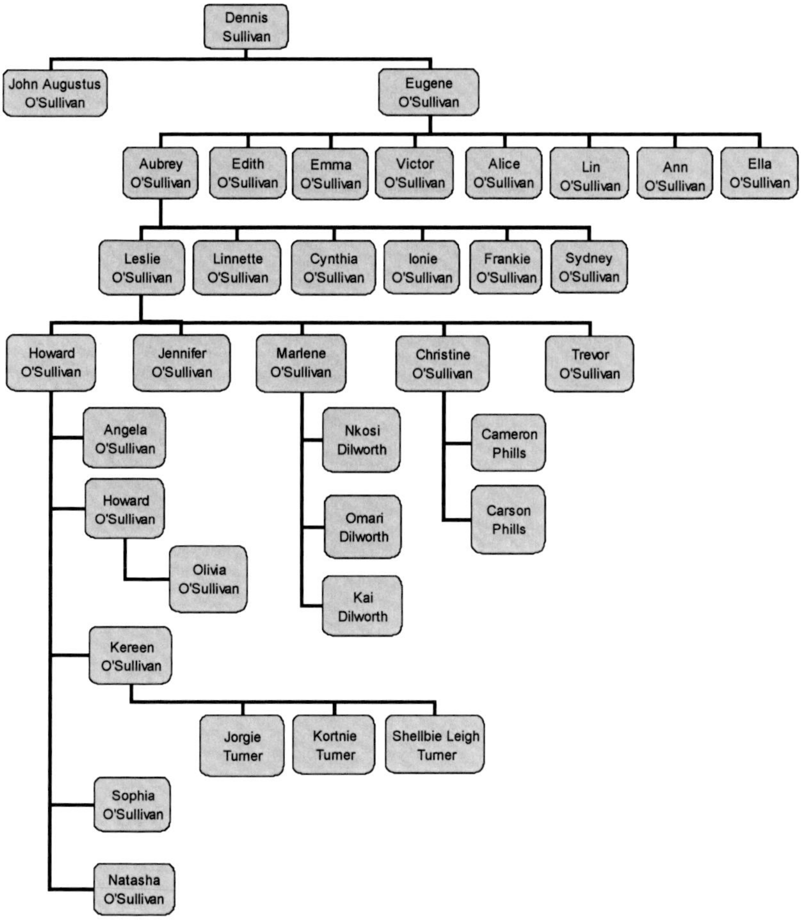

- a photo display of senior family members with name and relevant dates
- a 'memories' or 'Special Moments' family scrapbook of favourite expressions, quotes of family members and any other information you may wish to include
- a 'Family Address and Birthday' book adding photos to aid identification.
- an 'Index of Family Members' in alphabetical or date-of-birth order including parents' names, country of birth, places of residence at specific dates.
- a family tree computer programme.
- family stories, jokes, pastimes, other activities, experiences and achievements.

The time and energy you devote to the project, availability of material and cooperation of other family members will determine what you include.

1.6 Sharing the Information

There are several ways of sharing the information shown in the family tree/family tree package you have created.

- You could send out the family tree diagram and some/all notes in the form of a family newsletter. You could update it on a regular basis adding new information about the family.
- You could print note cards using family information – new members found, birth announcements, family photos, etc.
- You could arrange a family reunion or take advantage of a family 'get-together'.

No doubt you will have other ideas. The following suggestions for a family reunion are not exhaustive. They are based on experience and could prove helpful.

Family reunions

Family reunions or family 'get-togethers' may range from the simple to the sophisticated. They may be planned events or events such as christenings, weddings or anniversaries or may arise through unforeseen occasions like the death of a relative. Whatever the reason for the family coming together, some planning will ensure that things go well.

The following Family Reunion Checklist assumes long-term planning. However, some aspects of the checklist will be necessary, even when an unexpected family gathering is being organized. Bear in mind, it is better to have a short family reunion, with a few activities, than an elaborate one at which persons become bored or the cost becomes unaffordable to some.

Family reunion checklist

Before the reunion
1. Establish a planning committee (and subcommittees).
2. Define responsibilities of persons or subcommittees, e.g. communication, finance, programme organization (in-house), travel and accomodation logistics and organization of functions/outings.
3. Plan a schedule of meetings or teleconferences.
4. Solicit ideas from as many family members as possible even if they are not on a committee or subcommittee.

The planning stage
1. Choose a name or main theme for the reunion.
2. Plan the reunion programme – activities and timing of each. Schedule and indicate those for children, teenagers, young adults, the elderly, and those for all age groups.
3. Design a logo and get a banner made.
4. Compile a list of family members with addresses, telephone numbers, fax-numbers, e-mail addresses. Don't forget to include birthdays on the list for celebration at the event.

5. Select criteria for honouring family members.
6. Prepare guidelines to ensure everyone has a safe, memorable and enjoyable time.
7. Prepare a registration form designed to seek information about number of family members attending, number and ages of children, special health needs, etc.; and to seek information to fill any gaps that may exist in your research data on family members.
8. Make arrangements for emergency health needs and identify person(s) to be in charge
9. Make arrangements to record the event: identify photographer(s), video operator(s), tape recorder(s), journalist(s)/reporters(s)/ rapporteur(s).

Budgeting for expenses
1. Prepare a budget to include all expenses such as cost of services hired, stationery, telephone calls, music, certificates, prizes/awards, accommodation and group travel, electronic equipment and supplies.
2. Seek cash or kind contributions.
3. Fix a non-refundable registration fee. Decide amount to be prepaid and costs to be paid at reunion venue(s).

Contacting family members
1. Send out invitation packages well in advance of the reunion: Invitations should include date and location of reunion, programme of events, registration forms, costs, accommodation options, nearest airport, train or bus station.
2. Require and confirm pre-registration of family members.

After registration closes
1. Compile a list of family members attending the reunion.
2. Make up a list of persons attending each function/outing/ excursion.
3. Prepare name tags.

4. Prepare display of family tree/family history/other elements of the family package mentioned under section 1.5.

At the reunion

1. Establish a desk to welcome and record all arrivals to ensure that a tab may be kept on the group.
2. Request that guests wear name tags throughout the reunion. Consider giving all family members of one ancestor the same colour name tags. Name tags for small children should include names of parents, e.g. Kay (Parents: Maria and Michael Brown).
3. Celebrate birthdays that fall in the reunion period.
4. Confirm departure arrangements to ensure that family members are not left stranded.
5. Distribute printed copies or place on notice boards, revised schedules and other information. In addition, announce important arrangements at relevant times during the reunion.
6. Enquire daily if everyone is comfortable and appoint persons to receive and rectify complaints.
7. Use introductory activities to allow persons to get to know each other. The size of the group and the occasions will help to determine the types of activities which may be used.
8. Arrange to compile information from registration forms and information gathered at the reunion.
9. Discuss ways of maintaining contact after the reunion. This can include the collection of news about family members in the form of a 'family news bulletin'.
10. Solicit suggestions for the next reunion.

Post-reunion activities

Prepare statement of accounts and distribute to all families who attended along with 'thank-you' message and, perhaps, photo of family group under banner.

1.7 Other Reunions and Get-togethers

Other forms of reunions and get-togethers are becoming increasingly popular. They are based on the other institutional ties and bonds, and may well provide opportunities for family members to meet each other or at least, provide information about family members. Three such celebrations are identified below:

Parish homecomings

Some parish homecomings that have been held as annual events are those organized by St. Elizabeth, St. Thomas, St. Ann and Hanover.

Community homecomings

One example is that of the community homecoming held at Bleauwarie, in the parish of Westmoreland, in 1993. It was organized by members of the community living overseas. They all planned to come home at the same time and organized a number of activities to which local residents were invited.

Alumni homecomings

Alumni homecomings are organized by past students who live overseas, and are fast becoming popular as fund-raising activities. They have been held by primary school, secondary/high school, university and/or other professional institutions. Alumni homecomings also serve as occasions to renew old friendships/acquaintances, meet relatives and make new friends.

Compiling Your Family History

2.1 Further Research

Once you have completed your family tree, you already have some material for your family history. You are now ready to do further research and then to record your history. As with the family tree, you have to collect, organize and store information. In addition, you have to present the information in an interesting way.

Tips for compiling your family history

You should:
- decide what information you will include and make up a Table of Contents (you may need to change this as you get more information)
- begin writing your history with the oldest ancestor you can find and come forward to the present day
- be sure to highlight interesting and important ancestors and their achievements
- trace customs/trends in the family if there appear to be some. Illustrate with maps, photographs, printed materials (newspaper clippings, programmes from special events etc.).

Note: You may obtain information that you cannot share generally. Some information may have to be kept confidential until the person dies; even then, there may be family members who do not wish the information to be widely shared. Be sensitive and thoughtful of the feelings of others. Remember your objective is to build a cohesive family unit, not create divisions.

Sources of information

A variety of sources may be used to obtain information for your family history. Some are listed below:

Local sources
    Oral: See section 1.4.
    Written:
        Family or personal papers
        Church records
        Civil registration records
        Monumental inscriptions and cemetery records
        Military and naval records
        Public lists of awards
        Lists of public office holders
        Lists of educational achievements
        Newspapers, yearbooks, magazines and pamphlets
        Academic research
    Audio-visual:
        Radio programmes
        Internet sources
    Local places to obtain information

Overseas sources

2.2 Local Sources – Written

2.2.1 Family or personal papers

A listing of some important family papers which may be found in the possession of family members is given on the next page. They are documents to be kept when 'closing down' a family home. They are extremely valuable to the family historian. They contain priceless information about the lives of family members – their achievements, challenges and triumphs. This information provides insights into character and personality and strengthens the links between the past, present and future generations. Once destroyed or lost, the information may be lost forever or, at best,

difficult to retrieve.
- Birth, marriage and death certificates
- Family letters, photographs, drawings
- Family Bibles with their entries
- Job-related documents
- Court papers relating to disputes which went to court
- Newspaper clippings about family members
- Church programmes and /or magazines: Programmes include Order of Services for weddings, funerals, christenings, baptisms and programmes for anniversary celebrations, birthdays and other special occasions. Programmes often include names of participants, their roles at the function and their relationships to the person(s) for whom the event was organized
- Magazines and newsletters of organizations or associations to which family members belonged
- Business agreements, licences, letters
- Condolence cards
- Birth and marriage announcements
- Wedding invitations
- Commemorations (i.e. tributes, plaques, trophies, pins, brooches), citations (tributes) from work places, community or national organizations and social clubs tell of awards, achievements and contributions. They tell also of involvement in community organizations, indicate personal development of the recipient, as well as, changes in community life.
- Funeral eulogies: A eulogy is a tribute given at a funeral service that tells about the life and achievements of the deceased. The occasion of a funeral is a good time to collect family history. It is usually an occasion for the gathering of family and friends of the deceased. At this time of mourning many reminisce about the life and work of the deceased and talk about other family members with whom they have been acquainted.
- Medical reports: These may provide information that can guide the health care of younger family members. Diabetes and high blood pressure are two illnesses that are said to be hereditary. Early knowledge may help the young to observe healthy lifestyles.

- Educational documents: School reports and certificates are examples of educational documents. They may give clues to ages of individuals, locations in which they lived, as well as allowing development of profiles about their interests, achievements and skills.
- Legal documents relating to property: wills, probate papers, titles, survey diagrams, conveyances, tax receipts, common-law titles, mortgage agreements.

More about legal documents that may be in possession of families

Wills

Wills are documents prepared by individuals stating their wishes for disposal of property, valuables and cherished possessions after death. Wills provide financial information about the deceased and often the names and relationship of family members (the beneficiaries). Items left in a will have included land, furniture, jewellery, slaves, animals. A will also names person(s) responsible for carrying out the instructions (executor/executrix) of the will maker. A will may be kept at the home of the maker, given to a trusted individual for safe-keeping or left with a lawyer, bank or Registrar General's Department. On the death of the will-maker, the executor/executrix must get it probated (approved by the court) and then carry out the wishes of the deceased.

Today, all Jamaicans can make a will, but this was not always so. Prior to Emancipation, slaves were not allowed to make wills. Coloureds were not able to make wills until about the 1760s. Estate owners who were allowed to make wills sometimes granted freedom to favoured slaves and to their children born to slave women. In these wills, slaves were named.

After Emancipation, all people could make wills. Family property was often willed to sons or to male cousins, as on marriage a girl's inheritance became the property of her husband. Women who were widows did make wills. Married women were only allowed by law to make wills after the 1880s; before that all their property belonged to their husbands.

Many Jamaicans still do not make wills – they die intestate. In these cases, the government will issue a Letter of Administration authorizing someone of its choice to act as executor.

References

Mitchell, Madeleine E., *Alphabetical Index to Early Wills of Jamaica, 1655–1816*, PCC Wills 1655–1816 Registrar General's Office. Printed by Mino's, Pullman, Washington. e-mail: mitchel@pullman.com

Inventories and letters of guardianship

Persons who made wills may also have had other documents – Inventories and/or Letters of Administration concerning distribution of their property. Inventories listed non-land possessions of the deceased, the quantity and value of each item. Letters of Administration (adoms) showed the names of person(s) granted permission by the Governor or his representative to look about the property of the deceased.

Persons who make wills may also have inventories listing the possessions of the deceased, the quantity and value of each item. If a person dies intestate, government will obtain the inventory.

Indexes of Inventories, Letters of Administration, and Letters of Guardianship are available at the Registrar General's Office or at the National Archives.

Repositories of probated wills

Wills of Jamaicans who have lived in the island are to be found either in the island or in countries to which they migrated, or countries they came from.

Originals of wills are with the Supreme Court or the Registrar General's Department. In Jamaica, probated wills from 1663 are stored at the Registrar General's Department. The Administrator General may have copies of wills requiring their attention. They have a computerized data base, with files by name. They will be able to tell if they have copies of wills, but the search for copies may take some time.

Probated wills of persons who lived in Jamaica may also be found in the United Kingdom. Some of these wills are for persons who owned property in both places, or who went to the United Kingdom to live. Two locations where such wills may be deposited are:

- The Prerogative Court of Canterbury (PCC) for wills dated 1655–1858 available from the Public Record Office, United Kingdom (see section 2.5)

♚ The Court of Probate for wills after 1858 (see section 2.5)

Property titles, survey diagrams, conveyances, common-law titles and property tax receipts

Registered property titles

The original English colonists received land grants from the Crown. Ownership was established by a patent. At first patented land was limited to 300 acres, but this law was not always observed. The owners were entitled to will their land. If this was not done, the land reverted to the Crown. This is another word for the term widely used today — 'government land'. By 1828, most land was patented. Patent documents are in the National Archives, Spanish Town.

After 1838, many large holdings were subdivided for sale to ex-slaves, the new small farmers. Further subdivision of land has occurred under land settlement schemes, private development and government housing schemes.

The Registration of Titles Law 21 of 1888 came into operation on October 1, 1889. The manner of bringing land under the law is as follows:

> An application describing the lands, stating the value and giving the names of the persons in possession, and of the owners and occupiers of the adjoining lands is made on the printed form to be obtained from the Register to bring lands under the law and to have the certificate of title issued in the name of the applicant or in that of some other person.
> *Source: Handbook of Jamaica, 1906 p.24*

Where a title is registered under the law, the government guarantees the ownership of the land. Changes in ownership are recorded on the title so it becomes a valuable historical record.

Survey diagrams

Land Surveyors, at the request of the landowner or buyer, produce survey diagrams. The diagrams show the name of the landowner and the names of other parties interested in the survey. They are usually owners or occupants of adjoining lots. The diagram also gives the date of the survey, the size, shape and boundaries of the land being surveyed.

Common-law titles

These are documents stating that a piece of land belongs to a particular person. Ownership is established by word of mouth (i.e. agreed by neighbours) or by custom (person has lived continuously on the land for a specified number of years and has paid taxes on the property). A Common-Law Title can be changed to a Registered Title.

Conveyances

These are documents/agreements/deeds drawn up to transfer land from one person to another. They are used mainly in the case of Common-Law Titles.

Property tax

Government collects an annual tax on all property. The tax is payable at Collectorates. Most Collectorates are located in parish capitals, so some information about family land may be available there. A property tax receipt gives information regarding ownership, location, size, value of the land and the amount of taxes paid.

Since 1956 land valuation certificates have been issued by the Land Valuation Department – a government agency. Certificates show the name of the owner, the address of the property, the size of the holding and the value of the property at a particular date. The Land Valuation Department sends this information to the owner and also to the Collector of Taxes who calculates (assesses) the tax to be paid. The value of land is updated about every five years.

There are listings of properties 50 acres and upwards prepared by the Collector General for 1912, 1920 and 1938.

2.2.2 Church records

Church records are valuable sources of information on christenings, baptisms, marriages, deaths and burial places. These records include minutes of meetings, souvenir programmes and membership lists. Anniversary magazines may also contain information about individuals who made significant contributions to the work of the church. If you know the denomination to which your ancestor belonged, its records may offer some information.

Access to recent church records may require visits or correspondence to each denomination head office or to local churches. Use the telephone directory to make contact or write to the Minister/Pastor/Priest stating the information required. Some churches send historical records to their head offices, to the National Library and/or to the Archives.

Information relating to descendants of missionaries who came from overseas may be obtained from local and overseas head offices. The Congregational, Baptist, Presbyterian, Disciples of Christ, Moravian, Methodist are some of the denominations founded in Jamaica as overseas missions. Their records may mention the names of Jamaicans who were involved with their work. Jamaican head offices for each denomination may be able to supply information about their overseas founders.

Table 2.1 provides information to assist your family research. It gives the date of establishment of some Christian denominations and the address of their local headquarters.

Church of England (Anglican) registers

The Church-of-England Registers were kept on a parish basis. Because of this, it will be easier, when doing your research, if you know the parish(es) in which your ancestor(s) lived. However, remember that the present fourteen parishes were created in 1867, so, in earlier records, place names may be located in a different parish. If you know the location in which your ancestor resided, check the historical parish maps to ascertain the name of the parish at that date (see Appendix).

Remember too, that persons often resided in different parts of the same parish or moved from one parish to another. An individual could have been born in one parish, got married in another and then buried in still another parish. The individual may also have migrated to another country at some stage of his/her life. They may also have changed their residence in the new country. Table 2.2 shows parishes as they existed at various times.

The earliest Jamaican Church of England Registers began in 1666 and continued until 1870/1872. From 1668 to 1824, all birth, marriage and death registrations for each parish were kept in a

Compiling Your Family History

Table 2.1: Some Christian denominations, year established and Jamaican head offices

	Denomination	Year established	Head office in Jamaica
1.	Assemblies of God	1844	210 Mountain View Avenue, Kingston 6
2.	Baptist (Native) Baptist (English)	1782-83 (Leile & Baker) (USA) 1814	Jamaica Baptist Union, 6 Hope Road, Kingston 10
3.	Church of England (Anglican)	1655 (established as part of London Diocese) 1824 (Anglican Diocese of Jamaica created)	2 Caledonia Avenue, Kingston 5
4.	Church of God of Jamaica	1907	35 Hope Road, Kingston 10
5.	Congregational*	1834	12 Carlton Crescent, Kingston 10
6.	Disciples of Christ*	1858	12 Carlton Crescent, Kingston 10
7.	Jehovah's Witness	1897	Marliemont, Old Harbour P.O., Clarendon
8.	Methodist	1816	143 Constant Spring Road, Kingston 8
9.	Moravian	1754	3 Hector Street, Kingston 4
10.	New Testament Church of God	1925	9 Fairway Avenue, Kingston 5
11.	Presbyterian*	1824	12 Carlton Crescent, Kingston 10
12.	Roman Catholic	1494 (by the Spanish) 1792 re-established by French and Spanish immigrants	21 Hopefield Avenue, Kingston 6
13.	Salvation Army	1882	3 Waterloo Road, Kingston 10

*Joined to form the United Church in Jamaica and the Cayman Islands

Researching Your Jamaican Family

Table 2.2: Jamaican Parishes, 1664 to the present

1664	1683	1738	1844	1867 to present
Clarendon	Clarendon	Clarendon	Clarendon	Clarendon
		Hanover	Hanover	Hanover
		Kingston	Kingston	Kingston
			Manchester	Manchester
Port Royal	Port Royal	Port Royal	Metcalf	
		Portland	Portland	Portland
St. Andrew	St. Andrew	St. Andrew	St. Andrew	St. Andrew
		St. Annes	St. Ann	St.Ann
St. Katherin	St. Katherin	St. Catherine	St. Catherine	St. Catherine
St. David	St. David	St. David	St. David	
		St. Dorothy	St. Dorothy	St. Dorothy
	St. Elizabeth	St. Elizabeth	St. Elizabeth	St. Elizabeth
	St. Georges	St. George	St. George	
	St. James	St. James	St. James	St. James
St. John	St. John	St. John	St. John	
	St. Maries	St. Mary	St. Mary	St. Mary
St. Thomas ye East	St. Thomas ye East	St. Thomas in the East	St. Thomas in the East	St. Thomas
	St. Thomas ye Vale	St. Thomas in the Vale	St. Thomas in the Vale	
			Trelawney	Trelawny
	Vere	Vere	Vere	
		Westmoreland	Westmoreland	Westmoreland

parish book. After the creation of the Diocese of Jamaica in 1824 the parish priest sent information to the head office of the church in Spanish Town. The office then copied the information into separate all-island books under three categories: births, marriages, deaths.

Church-of-England Registers also contain records of non-Anglican persons. They were referred to as 'dissenters'; their records were classified as 'Dissenter Births', 'Dissenter Marriages' and 'Dissenter Deaths'. Presbyterian, Methodist, Baptist and Moravian are examples of dissenter denominations. Records of dissenters' births and deaths are for the period 1844 to 1854. There are also records for births, circumcisions, marriages, deaths and grave locations for Jews.

Before 1818, in order to be legal, marriages except those of Jews and Quakers had to take place in Anglican Churches. From 1818 onwards, persons were allowed to marry in other churches, but ministers performing the wedding ceremony had to send the information to the Anglican Bishop of Jamaica.

These Church of England Registers are available at the Island Records Office of the Registrar General's Department. Civil marriages (marriage by marriage officers other than clergymen) began in 1879. In summary, Church of England registers show:

- christening/baptism of infants, young children, adults
- marriage records
- burials conducted by the church, as well as the location of interment.

Church of Jesus Christ of the Latter-Day Saints

This church has records of over 250 million births, baptisms and marriages from around the world. Copies of these records, known as the International Genealogical Index (IGI) are available at the church's Family History Centre in Kingston and at their Family History Centres throughout the world. The centre in Jamaica has microfilm copies of:

1. Jamaican Anglican Church Parish Registers from the 1660s to 1800s. Surname death records began in 1878; surname marriage records began in 1871. The records include all dissenter records for the period 1844-1854.

2. Civil registration of births, deaths and marriages from the 1700s to 1930.

3. Jewish records of Jamaican births (1800s to 1950), circumcisions (1800s), marriages (1788-1920), deaths (1796-1824), grave registrations (about 1809-1850).

4. Wills from the Prerogative Court of Canterbury are on microfilm.

To use the facilities at the Family History Centre at 46-48 Gore Terrace, Kingston 10, Jamaica, West Indies, you should find out the opening hours, available information and details of the service offered.

Other church records

Older churches of all denominations may contain plaques on their walls (and in some cases, on the floor) as tributes to persons who made outstanding contributions. Furniture and fittings in the church may have small labels giving the names of donors and possibly, with a statement that the item was given in memory of an individual. At the sides of some church buildings are engraved stones with the names of those who made donations for the construction of the buildings. Older church members in a community are often very knowledgeable about past church members.

2.2.3 Civil registration records

Civil Registration Records are those required by Government. They give actual dates of births, marriages, deaths and burials.

An attempt at Civil Registration was made between 1844 and 1851. Only a few persons registered as required and so the law was revoked. Church of England records (Anglican) cover this period and they include dissenter records.

Between 1870 and 1880, Law 6 Registers recorded baptisms, marriages and burials of Anglicans and non-Anglicans (dissenters/non-conformists).

Compulsory registration of births and deaths was again instituted in April, 1878 and of marriages, in 1880.

Civil Registration Records were organized by parish. Each parish is divided into Registration Districts with each District having a Local Registrar. When individuals register births, marriages and deaths with a Local District Registrar, a number is assigned to each certificate. All registrations are sent to the head office of the Registrar General's Department where parish lists are compiled by surnames in alphabetical order.

Marriage certificates are batched at the Registrar General's Department according to the name of the Marriage Officer. Many Marriage Officers are Ministers of Religion. Knowing the name of the Marriage Officer and the number of the marriage certificate helps to expedite the search for a marriage certificate.

Other sources of birth, marriage and death records

- Estate records of some landowners
- Churches that keep christening, marriage and death registers for their own use
- Christening records may include the actual dates of birth, christening and names of parents and godparents
- Newspapers such as the *The Gleaner* (at one time called *Daily Gleaner*), the *Observer*, Royal Gazettes, the *Daily News*.

2.2.4 Monumental inscriptions and cemetery records

Monumental inscriptions are also valuable sources of information. They are inscriptions (writings) found on tombstones, on plaques in churches, on public buildings, on statues, cenotaphs / memorials and on cornerstones. The information obtainable depends on the type of monument, but will most likely include names and dates.

Burials may have taken place in family plots often located at the home of the deceased or other family member outside of towns. Burials also took place on estates where tombs of estate owners, their family members and management staff may have carried tombstones. It is possible that slave burial sites can be identified from estate maps.

Deceased church members may be interred in churchyard cemeteries or in public cemeteries. Many public cemeteries have sections for different denominations. Parish Council offices in each parish have responsibility for public cemeteries, but it is unlikely that the data is organized to allow easy access to the family historian. It would be best to arrange visits to public cemeteries after consultation with the relevant Parish Council and cemetery staff, family members or other persons familiar with the cemetery.

Tombstone inscriptions usually show names, dates of birth and death, and some relatives. Some even give the cause of death. Religious quotations, a cross or other drawings adorn many tombstones. Take note of the type of tombstone material – is it local material or imported material? Note also the style of the artwork; it can be helpful in dating and also in indicating social standing.

Cremation started in Jamaica in the 1960s. Ashes may be

interred in family plots, churchyards, public cemeteries or in locations requested by the deceased. Very few persons are buried at sea.

Funeral directors may assist with information about the deceased, if some of the following information is supplied:
- name of the deceased
- date of death
- date of burial
- place of burial

The level of assistance may vary, as most funeral homes may not yet have computerized the data.

There are some special cemeteries in Jamaica. Here are some:
- Military cemeteries at Up Park Camp and Port Royal in Kingston, and at Newcastle in the hills of St. Andrew
- Jewish cemeteries at Hunt's Bay and Orange Street in Kingston; Spanish Town in St. Catherine, Montego Bay in St. James, Falmouth in Trelawny, Lucea in Hanover. Other places with Jewish tombstones are Lacovia and Alligator Pond in St. Elizabeth, Savanna-la-mar in Westmoreland, Annotto Bay in Portland, St. Ann's Bay in St. Ann, Gaza, Watson Hill and Rowe's Corner in Manchester and Port Maria in St. Mary. Older Jewish tombstones have inscriptions in Portuguese and Spanish.

Cenotaph memorials listing those who died in World Wars I and II are located in some parish capitals. Examples include:
- Westmoreland – the cenotaph is located in Norman Square, Savanna-la-mar
- Kingston & St. Andrew – a plaque listing the names of former residents of both parishes who died was mounted on the clock tower in Cross Roads, St. Andrew, on October 11, 1956
- St. James – Montego Bay Anglican churchyard
- Portland – Port Antonio
- St. Thomas – Morant Bay, near the courthouse
- St. Mary – Claude Stuart Park, Port Maria

References

Archer, Lawrence & Henry, James, *Monumental Inscriptions of the*

British West Indies. Chatto and Windus London, 1875.
Bailey, Betty, with photographs by Ernest deSouza, 'Tombstones in the Jewish Cemetery and What They Tell' in *Jamaica Journal* Vol. 2, No. 2, 1987. Institute of Jamaica Publications Ltd.
Barnett R. D. & Wright, P., *The Jews of Jamaica: Tombstone Inscriptions 1663-1880*. Jerusalem Zvi Institute, 1997.
Coulthard, G. R., 'Inscriptions on Jewish Gravestones' in *Jamaica Journal* Vol. 2, March, 1968. Institute of Jamaica Publications Ltd.
Langford, Oliver. *The Monumental Inscriptions of the British West Indies.* Vere Dorchester F. G. Longman The Friary Press, 1927.
Roby, John, Monuments of the Cathedral Church and Parish of St. Catherine being Part I of Church Notes and Monumental Inscriptions of Jamaica in the year 1824 published privately in Montego Bay.
St. Andrew Parish Church Burial Register and Listings of Selected Inscriptions (1669–1994 but excluding the years 1900–1947) a volunteer project headed by David Lindo.
Wright, Philip, *Monumental Inscriptions of Jamaica (1655–1880)*. Society of Genealogists, London, 1996.

2.2.5 Military, naval and police records

Military records for the island date from the Spanish and British conquests. Records for Spanish ancestors would be in Spain, and those for the English are primarily in England with a few in Jamaica.

Categories of military records

Jamaica Militia records 1662-1906

The Jamaica Militia predated the formation of a police force. Militias were made up of male, white local landowners and later free coloureds. Militias were organized to protect the island from foreign attacks, and to quell Maroon and slave uprisings. They were organized on a parish basis and on a county basis – Cornwall, Middlesex and Surrey.

At its maximum strength, in the early nineteenth century, there were:

> 10,000 infantry and 1,000 cavalry divided between 3 regiments of horse, one for each county and 18 regiments on foot, one for each of the then eighteen parishes of Jamaica – and commanded at one time by no less than four Major Generals.

Source: Historical Overview of the Jamaica Defence Force Website, September 2002

British Royal Artillery and Navy records

Men for these regiments came to or were raised in Jamaica from the time of the American Revolutionary War 1775 to the beginning of Jamaica's Independence in 1962. Early regiments were named after commanders. Later regiments were numbered, for example, the 60th Regiment and the 92nd Regiment.

Descendants born of British soldiers and naval officers may find records in:

- Jamaican birth, marriage and death records especially Church of England Registers for towns near to forts and army barracks
- Military cemeteries in Jamaica (see page 30)
- Churches, especially Anglican Churches, close to towns and forts may have tombstones and plaques with inscriptions about military and naval personnel
- Estate burial grounds may also have tombstones with inscriptions
- British military and naval records in England through the Public Record Office (see section 2.5 for address)
- Jamaica Legion (formerly the Veterans' Association), Curphey Place, Kingston 5. Tel: (876) 926-2382
- Jamaica Militia Records 1662-1907.

Jamaican military service records

Records for some persons may be found in British records and in the records of the Jamaica Defence Force (JDF). JDF records go back to World War II (1939-44).

JDF has two types of records:

- Those for military personnel
- Those for civilian personnel

Inquiries should state whether the person was a soldier or a civilian. A soldier's rank and number would assist the search.

Address: The Headquarters
           The Jamaica Defence Force
           Up-Park-Camp, Kingston 5
           Jamaica, West Indies

Telephone: (876) 926-8121 (General)
           (876) 960-5362 (Records)

Police records

Researchers looking for information on family members who served in the internal security forces should note that formation of a police force dates from an Act of 1832. Prior to the formation of the Force, the function of internal security and maintenance of law and order was the responsibility of the Jamaica Militia. Composition of the force by rank in 1856 is given in the historical notes of section 4.2: Defence, Law & Order.

The Police Academy in Spanish Town, the Archives in Spanish Town, the National Library and the Administrative Branch (Police) at 101 Old Hope Road, Kingston 6, Jamaica, West Indies are sources of information.

Records at the Police Headquarters date from the late 1920s. Inquires should give the name, age and address(es) of officers, places stationed, and ranks.

Police promotions are usually placed in the *Jamaica Gazette*.

Earlier records of overseas (British) police personnel are available in the United Kingdom.

2.2.6 Lists of public awards

Every year people are nominated and chosen to receive various awards. Lists of these awards may well include members of your immediate family and/or of your ancestors, so it is well worth your while to get hold of them and examine them. Below are some examples of public awards.

National honours and awards

The bestowing of National Honours and Awards (National Honours and Award Act, 1969) is conducted, annually, in October by the Governor General at King's House. Awardees are nominated by members of the public and further selected by a committee, the Chancery of the Orders of the Societies of Honour, at King's House. Posthumous awards are sometimes given. The major newspapers usually publish lists. Categories of awards are:

The Order of National Hero
The Order of the Nation (ON)
The Order of Merit (OM)
The Order of Jamaica (OJ)

The Order of Distinction – in the rank of Commander (CD)
The Order of Distinction – in the rank of Officer (OD)
The Badge of Honour for Gallantry (BHG)
The Badge of Honour for Meritorious Service (BHM)
The Badge of Honour for Long and Faithful Service (BHL)
The Medal of Honour (Uniformed Services)
The Badge of Honour (Civilians)

Before Jamaica instituted National Awards, Jamaicans were eligible for British awards granted annually by the British Monarchy when Jamaica was a colony. Awardees were recommended by the Governor and then, by the Governor-General after the island became independent. British awards were replaced by Jamaican National Honours in 1969.

Musgrave Medal

This medal was introduced in 1889 in memory of Sir Anthony Musgrave, a former Governor of the island and founder of the Institute of Jamaica. The award is given in recognition of outstanding contributions to Literature, Science and the Arts. Awards are presently made in the month of October.

Jamaica Civil Service Long Service Awards

Presentation of these awards began in 1988 for 30 years of service. Since 1994, the length of service was reduced to 25 years.

Governor-General's Achievement Awards

These are awards for commitment to community development. They are granted, on a parish basis, to outstanding individuals. These awards were established in 1992.

2.2.7 Lists of public office holders

The names of public office holders are usually published in newspapers and in the Jamaica Gazette. Early lists are stored at the National Archives, some of them in minutes of Vestry meetings (local government committee that met in the Vestry of the Church of England). The lists include:

Justices of the Peace
Members of Parliament and Senators
Members of Parish Councils
Members of Government Boards
Members of Statutory Boards
Members of Government Commissions

2.2.8 Lists of educational attainments

These include lists of scholarships and awards at all levels (government and private), examination results and placements in secondary schools. Some have been published in newspapers. Lists for secondary schools state the full names of students, schools from which they wrote the examination and their new schools. This information can be very valuable to the family historian.

Other sources are the Overseas Examination Office, the Caribbean Examination Council, the Ministry of Education, the National Library, University attended by the family/ancestor(s).

Some schools have lists of their scholars on display boards and also report them in school magazines and yearbooks.

Publications by educational institutions with information about individuals include yearbooks and graduation lists. Examples include publications and programmes from secondary schools, teachers' colleges, theological colleges, professional schools and universities.

Lists of university graduates, recipients of bursaries, scholarships and grants are available at local universities. Name of graduate, campus attended, faculty enrolled in, year entered and year of graduation should be supplied. Addresses of some universities are:

- The Registrar, University of the West Indies, Mona, Kingston 7, Jamaica, West Indies.
- The Office of Admissions and Records, Northern Caribbean University, Mandeville P.O., Manchester, Jamaica, West Indies (formerly West Indies Training College).
- The University of Technology, 237 Old Hope Road, Kingston 6, Jamaica, West Indies (formerly, the College of Arts, Science and Technology – CAST).

2.2.9 Newspapers, yearbooks, magazines, pamphlets

Many newspapers have birth, engagement, marriage, anniversaries and death announcements and memorials columns. See section 2.4.3 for listings of newspaper titles and where to find back issues.

The *Gleaner* newspaper carries requests from persons seeking information on family members on its "Letters to the Editor" page.

Families whose ancestors have lived in a specific location for generations should seek documented information – records of community-based organizations such as churches, schools, estates and agricultural associations. Records may include minutes of meetings to which persons belong(ed) and to which they made significant contributions. Some community-based organizations publish magazines, newsletters, etc.

Telephone directories

Telephone service commenced in Jamaica in the late 1880s. This was just two years after Bell invented the telephone. The oldest telephone directory held by the National Library is dated 1927 – a temporary directory for Kingston. Back copies for other years are available at the National Library.

2.2.10 Academic research

Jamaican and other international historians have researched and published information on the social, economic and political development of Jamaica. The role of the local population in this development is still being researched.

Records for the period 1492-1834 (Pre-emancipation period) are primarily those of colonial governments, landowners, religious groups, merchants and newspapers. Examples of these include estate documents, ship lists of persons who travelled from British ports, lists of persons arriving in the island, listings of civil servants, tax rolls, slave and manumission (freedom) lists. Some of these are obtainable in Jamaica and others are overseas. Spanish records are in Spain; those for the English period are in England. Local records are in the archives, government departments, libraries, museums and private collections.

Prior to 1834 very little information would have been recorded by the slaves themselves as only a few were able to read and write. After Emancipation in 1838, as the number of educated free people increased, and as they began to participate in more varied aspects of the society, so did documentation about them.

All this makes it possible for the family historian to have access to names of persons and places in written records. Consult the reference lists given in this text to aid your research.

Note: There are many categories of reference material. It all depends on what you are seeking. Use library catalogues, indexes to material, tables of content and documents to help you to define your research pathways.

2.3 Local Sources – Audio-Visual

The family historian should always be on the lookout for programmes that can provide insights and information on our ancestors. Some of these are:

Radio programmes
- 'Sunday Contact' – on Radio Jamaica AM that invites persons wishing to make contact with family and friends to write or call the programme.
- 'Children of the Dragon' – on News Talk 93 FM tells about the history and culture of the Chinese.
- 'Indian Talent on Parade'– on Power 106 FM promotes Indian music and culture.

Internet websites
Examples include those listed by the National Library and the *Gleaner* newspaper.

2.4 Local Places to Obtain Information

Places in Jamaica listed below are those most likely to have information of interest to family historians. There is, however, no guarantee that they will be able to supply all the information needed. This is so because family research has not been done on a large scale in Jamaica. Few places with information have the material computerized or organized to facilitate this type of research. The family historian may, therefore, have to do a lot of searching themselves. In some cases, access to materials will have to be discussed with the administration of the particular place.

- The Registrar General's Department (RGD)
- The Jamaica Archives and Records Department
- The National Library and other libraries
- Courts
- Government offices
- The Jamaica National Heritage Trust
- Museums and historical societies

2.4.1 The Registrar General's Department (RGD)

The Registrar General's Department (RGD) has two sections:
- The General Register Office, and
- The Island Records Office.

The General Register Office

The General Register Office registers births, marriages and deaths. It keeps all records relating to registrations. All of these records are important to family research. These records are of two types:
- Church of England (Anglican) Registers (see section 2.2.3).
- Civil Registration required by Government which includes all ethnic and religious groups (see section 2.2.3).

Certified and uncertified copies of birth, marriage, and death certificates are available. The information certificates supply are shown in Table 2.3.

Table 2.3: Information on birth, marriage and death certificates

Birth certificate	Marriage certificate	Death certificate
Name of person	Name of groom	Name of deceased
Name of mother	Maiden name of bride	Place and parish of death
Name of father	Place of marriage	Date of death and cause of death
Date of birth	Date of marriage	
Place of birth	Name of marriage officer	Sex of deceased
Whether adopted or not	Witnesses to the wedding	Date of registration of death
		Place of registration of death

Note: Each certificate has a registration number which is necessary for tracing information.

The Island Record Office

The Island Record Office houses a Genealogical Research Department which is open to the family historian. The department records include:

- Adoption certificates
- Bills of sale with liens
- Certificates of citizenship
- Conveyances
- Laws of Jamaica
- Naturalization papers
- Parish Registers (baptisms, marriages, burials)
- Powers of attorney
- Wills and Deeds from 1660 to the present (probated copies of wills of the Resident Magistrate Court from 1663 and from the Supreme Court from 1880)

Current charges are per generation, per Family Tree and per birth, marriage and death certificates per family member found.

Process time: Regular Service, Express Service

Service cost: Cost depends on the type of documentation and processing requested. Ordinary and courier services are available. Overseas customers should pay by International Money Order or British Postal Order.

The information needed by the Genealogical Research Department for tracing a family history is:

- names of family members (there may be spelling variations; watch out for them)
- dates of births, marriages, deaths
- names of brothers, sisters, other relatives
- names of spouses
- names of children
- occupations
- places and parishes of residence

There is also an hourly fee for use of records.

    Address: The Registrar General Department
                     Twickenham Park,
                     Spanish Town P.O., St. Catherine
                     Jamaica, West Indies
    Telephone: (876) 984-3041-5
    Toll Free: 1-888-rgd-care (1-888-743-2273)
    Fax: (876) 984-2353
    Website: *www.rgd.gov.jm*
    e-mail: information@rgd.gov.jm

Opening hours: Monday to Thursday 8.30 a.m. to 5.00 p.m.
Friday 8.30 a.m. to 4.00 p.m.

2.4.2 The Jamaica Archives and Records Department

The Jamaica Archives and Records Department keeps primarily public records. Examples of these include:

- Parish Registers (baptisms, marriages, burials)
- Patents of Land Grants 1661-1940
- Plats (drawings of land grants) 1661-1755
- Registers of slaves and manumissions

    Address: The Jamaica Archives and Records Department
                     King and Manchester Streets,
                     Spanish Town P.O., St. Catherine
                     Jamaica, West Indies
    Telephone: (876) 984-2581

Opening hours: Mondays to Fridays 9.00 a.m. to 3.00 p.m.

Materials available: Certified copies of documents for a fee.

Charge for service: A search fee is charged by the hour.

2.4.3 The National Library and other libraries

The National Library was established in 1979. The library incorporated the collection of the former West India Reference Library (WIRL) which was established in 1894 as a division of the Institute of Jamaica.

The library collects and preserves material about Jamaica. The collection includes material produced by Jamaicans and non-Jamaicans, locally and overseas.

The information found here will most likely be on persons who have made outstanding contributions to community and national life.

Services offered: Assistance with reference searches; Research assistance at a fee; Photocopying at a fee; Reproduction of maps and photographs at a fee.

In addition to books, the National Library offers the following materials which may provide valuable information for the family historian:

- business directories
- yearbooks and handbooks
- maps and prints
- manuscripts
- newspapers, newspaper clippings, pamphlets and special supplements about schools, other institutions, towns, cities, businesses
- annual reports
- collections of films, tapes, CD's, phonograph records, photos, programmes of educational, cultural and sporting events, slides, video cassettes.

Business directories

- *Commercial Handbooks of Jamaica 1911–*
- *DeSouza's Commercial Handbook and Business Directory 1916–*
- *Times Commercial Directory 1910–*, by H.M. Cornish, Kingston

Yearbooks and handbooks

- *Directory of Jamaican Personalities* started in the 1980s continues to the present.
- *Handbook of Jamaica* – an annual publication 1881–1971 with the exception of 1940–1945 (war years). These handbooks offer a wide range of listings e.g. 1895 edition has a list of passes in the Local & Cambridge external examinations, schools attended and their headmasters. The 1966 edition includes a listing of Barristers-at-law, Justices of the Peace, members of boards and associations, names, posts and salaries of public servants, information on trade and commerce, secondary schools, ecclesiastical and religious information.
- *The Jamaica Almanack* commenced publication in 1672. Later, the name was changed to the *Jamaica Almanac*. It was an annual publication from 1776–1879. Editions from the late 1770s included information on Jamaica and persons in the island. A range of topics was covered, with listing of persons associated with organizations and public offices. Names of individuals are listed under Parish headings.
- *The Jamaica Journal* – a magazine published by the Institute of Jamaica containing articles on various aspects of Jamaican life and culture.
- *Personalities Caribbean* was a Caribbean biography started in 1960s. Jamaicans are listed with other Caribbean personalities.
- *Reference of Jamaica B.W.I.* contains information on professional directory, Art and Culture, Recreation and Sports, Private Nursing Homes, Honours Lists, Business Directory, with photographs of business places and individuals. Edited and published by Wyatt Bruce, Kingston 1946.
- *Who's Who in Jamaica* – a publication of outstanding citizens produced from 1916 to 1976 at approximately four year intervals. Photographs are included. Information includes names, dates of birth, names of parents, spouses, children, occupations.

Maps and prints

The map collection consists of maps showing boundaries of land deeds, boundaries of patents with names of owners and adjacent owners, details of estate layout, plots assigned to slaves, their names and their mothers' names.

Manuscripts

These include unpublished diaries, correspondences, estate and other records.

Newspapers, newspaper clippings, special supplements

Dating from 1718, Jamaican newspapers number over 200. Jamaican newspapers, including microfilm copies, may be accessible from libraries throughout the world. Some early newspapers served small towns or areas while others are national in outlook. Examples of towns that offered most newspapers are shown in Table 2.4.

Table 2.4: A sample of newspapers offered by towns

Town	Date started	Newspaper
Kingston		
	1780	*The Royal Gazette*
	1834	*The Gleaner*, 1902 name changed to *The Daily Gleaner*, December 1992 name changed to *The Gleaner*.
	1950	*Chung San News* – published twice weekly in Chinese
	1849	*The Colonial Standard*
	December 1894	*The Jamaica Advocate* – a weekly newspaper started by Robert Love
	1930	*Chinese Public News* – twice weekly, partly in Chinese
	February 20, 1937 to April 4, 1944	*Public Opinion* – a weekly
Spanish Town		
	1756	*St. Jago Gazette*
	1757	*The St. Jago Intelligence*
	1801	*The St. Jago de la Vega Gazette*
Montego Bay		
	1776	*Cornwall Chronicle*
	1883	*The 19th Century & St. James Gazette*
	1947	*The Montego Bay Times*

Town Date started	Newspaper
Falmouth	
1832	Cornwall Courier
1835	Falmouth Post
1885	Falmouth Gazette
1918	The Trelawny
1918	The Northern News and Provincial

Many of the earlier newspapers served the interests of the estate owners and merchants. Newspapers catering to the free coloured population before the end of slavery included:

- *The Watchman* and *Jamaica Free Press* started by Edward Jordan and Robert Osborne in 1829

Some of those of the Post-Emancipation period served the interests of coloureds and blacks; they survived for shorter periods.

- *The Morning Journal* started by Robert Gordon also served the population later in the nineteenth century
- *The Jamaican Advocate* was founded by Dr. Robert Love, a black Bahamian, in 1894 after *The Gleaner* refused to publish his letters. Dr. Love lived in the United States of America and in Central America before making Jamaica his home. His newspaper was an outlet for issues relating to black people. He encouraged them to be educated, to develop self esteem and to take pride in themselves and their African heritage.
- Marcus Garvey published the following:
  The Blackman 1929–1931, first as a daily and then as a weekly
  The New Jamaican, an evening daily, July 1932 – Sept. 1933
  Blackman, a magazine, near the end of 1933 to 1939

Newspaper clippings are compiled by the library under various headings. This is usually an ongoing activity.

Annual reports

Annual reports are often put out by business companies, professional and other associations and societies.

Collection of audio-visuals

These are also available from the Jamaica Information Service (JIS), Jamaica Archives and Records Department, media houses, and from private sources.

    Address: The National Library
                       12 East Street, Kingston
                       Jamaica, West Indies
    Telephone: 967-2494
    Website: *www.nlj.org.jm*
    Opening hours: Mondays to Thursdays 9.00 a.m. to 5.00 p.m.
                                Fridays 9.00 a.m. to 4.00 p.m.

Other libraries

These include Parish Libraries, Libraries in Government Offices (e.g. Jamaica Tourist Board, Ministry of Agriculture, Planning Institute of Jamaica). The University of the West Indies offers a West Indian Reference Section. Contact these libraries prior to visiting to make arrangements to use their facility.

The Library of *The Gleaner* offers access to material and sells copies of photographs in its publications. Microfilm copies of *The Gleaner* and *The Daily Gleaner* from 1865–1940 are available. The library is accessible by appointment on Tuesdays and Wednesdays from 9.00 a.m. to 4.00 p.m. There is a library pass fee. The first hour of assisted research is free with an hourly charge thereafter.

Online access to *The Gleaner* Archive and Library Service is viz *www.jamaica-gleaner.com*. Copies of *The Gleaner* from October 28, 1988 are available on its archive website.

2.4.4 Courts

Court records may give some information on family matters and on individual family members. Many persons use the courts to settle disputes over possessions – especially family land, disputes among family members, conflicts between strangers, companies or organizations. Court records also relate to legalizing changes such as adoptions, child protection and divorces. There are also records of those who committed crimes.

Newspapers carry reports of some court cases. These may involve well-known persons and unusual and serious offences.

Knowledge of the year(s) of trial, names of persons involved would help to guide the research.

Older court records are available at the Archives, the Registrar General's Department and at Parish Court houses. Procedures to obtain access to these vary with each institution. Records of cases that went to higher courts in England, such as the Privy Council, would be available there.

Names and types of courts have changed over the years and some may no longer exist. You will need to ascertain types of courts in the time frame you are researching. Between 1655 and 1838 the following were types of courts:

- The Court of Chancery
- The Jamaica Supreme Court
- The Jamaica Grand Court or Court of Error
- The Court of the Ordinary
- Assizes Courts

In 1844 Courts were listed as follows:

- Court of Chancery
- Court of Appeal and Errors
- The Court of the Ordinary
- The Court of the Supreme Judicature
- The Court of Assize, Oyer and Terminer
- The Court of Assize Nisi Prius
- The Court of the Vice-Admiralty
- The Court of the Admiralty Session
- The Court of Quarter Sessions
- The Court of Common Pleas (one in each parish)
- The Court of the Justices of the Peace in Petty Sessions

Source: The Political Constitution of Jamaica – its Annual Laws in force for 1844.

Note: No court had the power to grant divorces.

The 2006 Telephone Directory lists the following courts:

- The Court of Appeal
- The Family Court
- The Gun Court
- The Juvenile Court
- The Kingston Civil Division
- The Kingston Criminal Division

- The Resident Magistrate's Courts (in Kingston and some parishes)
- The Revenue Court
- The Supreme Court
- The Traffic Court

Other sources of information of interest to the family historian may be available at the Law Faculty at the University of the West Indies, Mona, Jamaica. A search of books of Jamaican court cases and lawyers may yield some results. For example, Jackie Ranston in *First Time Up* chronicles the career of lawyer Norman Manley and contains references to law cases in which he was involved.

2.4.5 Government offices

Some government offices may have information that can be useful to the family historian. Some have libraries, research departments or public relations departments. Much depends on the nature and date of the information you want and the level of staff consulted.

Before visiting these offices use the telephone directory and seek to make contact and an appointment with someone who may assist.

Historical material may be found (and lodged) with the Jamaica Archives and Island Records Department, National Library, the Registrar General's Department and the Jamaica Information Service (JIS) in Kingston.

Government offices with responsibilities for matters relating to land ownership

Government offices dealing with land ownership have all been combined under a single agency – The National Land Agency. The corporate office is located at:

Address: 8 Ardenne Road, Kingston 10, Jamaica, West Indies
Telephone: (876) 750-5263, (876) 946-5263
e-mail: asknla@nla.gov.jm
Website: **www.nla.gov.jm**

The offices are as follows:
- Business Service Centre
  23½ Church Street, Kingston, Jamaica, West Indies

- Estate Management Division
  Corporate Legal Services Division
  20 North Street, Kingston, Jamaica, West Indies
- Land Titles Division / Office of Titles
  93 Hanover Street, Kingston, Jamaica, West Indies
- The Land Valuation Department, Corporate Office
  8 Ardenne Road, Kingston 10, Jamaica, West Indies
- Survey and Mapping Division
  23½ Church Street, Kingston, Jamaica, West Indies

The **Estate Management Division** manages lands owned by the Commissioner of Lands. The job includes the purchase of land for public purposes and the management of land settlement schemes.

The **Land Titles Division** holds land titles and records all transactions about a piece of land. You may go there to examine original titles. There is also a photocopying service.

The function of the **Land Valuation Department** was described on page 23. In addition to the main office which serves the southern region, there are two regional offices:

Central Region

5½ Caledonia Road
G1-G6 Golf View Shopping Centre
Mandeville P.O.Manchester
Jamaica, West Indies

Western Region

3 Federal Avenue
Montego Bay
St. James
Jamaica, West Indies

The **Survey and Mapping Division** surveys land and produces a variety of maps for the entire island. You may purchase sections of these maps which are of interest to you. Maps are available at different scales. Aerial black and white photographs are also available.

2.4.6 The Jamaica National Heritage Trust

This organization has responsibility for the care and preservation of all national monuments and historic sites in the island. These sites are being protected for the benefit of the people of Jamaica. Sites and monuments are protected by the Trust on the basis of their historic, architectural, aesthetic, traditional, scientific or archaeological interest. The Trust also provides information on these sites and the family historian may wish to consult them about

those that may be relevant to their family.
Address: The Jamaica National Heritage Trust
Headquarters House
79 Duke Street, Kingston
Jamaica, West Indies
Telephone: (876) 922-1287 / (876) 922-1288
Fax: (876) 967-7170-3

2.4.7 Museums and historical societies

Museums and historical societies in the area in which your ancestors lived may provide information on your family and their community which may help you to build a picture of their life style. You may even be 'lucky enough' to make contact with other relatives while researching your family history.

Museums

Following is a list of museums which you may find useful:

- Accompong Community Museum
  Accompong, St. Elizabeth, Jamaica, West Indies
- The African-Caribbean Institute of Jamaica
  – Jamaica Memory Bank
  1 Ocean Boulevard, Kingston, Jamaica, West Indies
- The Bank of Jamaica Museum (exhibiting history of money)
  Nethersole Place, Kingston, Jamaica, West Indies
- The Forces' Museum
  Up-Park-Camp, Kingston 5, Jamaica, West Indies
- German Museum
  Seaford Town, c/o Sacred Heart Mission, Lamb's River
  Westmoreland, Jamaica, West Indies
- Hanover Historical Society and Museum
  The Barracks, P.O.Box 35, Lucea,
  Hanover, Jamaica, West Indies
- The Institute of Jamaica
  12 East Street, Kingston, Jamaica, West Indies

- Mico College Museum (a collection of African artifacts)
  la Marescaux Road, Kingston 5, Jamaica, West Indies
  College records prior to 1950 are at the National Library and those after 1950 are held at the college.
- People's Museum of Craft and Technology
  Spanish Town, St. Catherine, Jamaica, West Indies
- Port Royal Museum
  Port Royal, Jamaica, West Indies
- Seville Great House and Heritage Park
  (a collection of Taino, Spanish and English artifacts)
  St. Ann's Bay, St. Ann, Jamaica, West Indies
- Taino Museum
  White Marl, Spanish Town,
  St. Catherine, Jamaica, West Indies
- Taino Museum
  University of the West Indies, Mona, Kingston 7, Jamaica, West Indies

Historical Societies

- The Georgian Society of Jamaica
  58 Half-Way-Tree Road, Kingston 10,
  Jamaica, West Indies
- The Jamaica Historical Society
  58 Half-Way-Tree Road, Kingston 10,
  Jamaica, West Indies

  This society publishes a bulletin twice a year and the 'Jamaican Historical Review' every two years. An index of articles is available at the National Library.
- Jamaica Jewish Genealogical Society
  58 Paddington Terrace, Kingston 6, Jamaica, West Indies
  www.jewishgen.org

List of Jamaican genealogy material

Books

- *Genealogy of Jamaica. An aid to Research on Jamaican Families.* Compiled by Donald Lindo. First edition July 1998. P.O. Box 493, Halfway Tree, Kingston 10, Jamaica, West Indies   E-mail: deal@colis.com
- Mitchell, Madeleine E. *Alphabetical Index to Early Wills of Jamaica, 1655-1816*, PCC Wills 1655-1816 Registrar General's Office Printed by Mino's, Pullman, Washington. e-mail: mitchel@pullmna.com
- Mitchell Madeleine E. *Jamaican Ancestry: How to Find Out More.* Heritage books. Inc. Maryland, USA. 1988. ***www.heritagebooks.com***.
- Registrar General's Department. *Genealogical Handbook.* Pear Tree Press Ltd., 2003.

2.5 Overseas Sources

Contact overseas family members to gain information. These persons may have letters giving accounts of the family in Jamaica, and other memorabilia collected over the years. Photographs and paintings would be those of family members.

You may wish to research your ancestors in their countries of origin or the countries to which they migrated.

Increasingly information relating to Jamaican Genealogy is appearing on overseas Genealogy websites. There is information on family trees and family histories (often posted by family members), Jamaican history (reference material) and chat-rooms. Relevant websites can also be found on Jamaica's National Library website. Information on Jamaican and other Caribbean family histories is available on ***www.cyndislist.com/hispanic.htm***.

You may also wish to contact specific organizations such as:

- The Federation of Family History Societies
  P.O. Box 2425
  Coventry CY5 6YX
  England

Researching Your Jamaican Family

The Public Records Office in England also supplies information useful to family historians. It has two offices:

- Public Record Office
  Kew, Ruskin Avenue
  Richmond, Surrey TW9 4DW
  England   Website: ***www.pro.gov.uk***
- Family Records Centre
  Myddleton Street
  London EC1R 1UW
  England   Website: ***www.familyrecords.gov.uk***

The address for the Court of Probate for wills after 1858 (as mentioned on page 22) is:

- Principal Registry Office, Probate Department
  Principal Registry of the Family Division
  First Avenue House
  42-49 High Holborn
  London WC1V 6NP
  England

# 3

Ethnic Roots of Jamaican Families

The ethnicity of a family will determine some of the material to be used to research its early history.

While a majority of Jamaicans are of African descent, many families are a mixture of different ethnic and racial groups. Included in any one family may be persons of African, European, Indian, Chinese and Lebanese (Syrian) descent – visibly discernible or not (see map 2 on next page). Our Jamaican motto, crafted at the time the island became independent from Britain in 1962, recognizes this diversity of racial and ethnic groups. These immigrants account for Jamaica's culture. They have created the hallmark of the Jamaican society and have given the nation a distinctly Jamaican identity – different groups of persons, living in harmony, and inspiring the motto which embodies their hopes and dreams of a people united:

Out of many, one people

Each generation of immigrant groups (colonizers, slaves, indentured and non-indentured groups) have Jamaicanized/creolized the culture of their ancestors. Traditional practices of family life, food, dress, music, festivals and religion have all been affected. Indentured and other immigrants who came after Emancipation retained more of their cultural heritage than Africans who came as slaves. But those immigrants also found that they had to adopt many of the existing social norms of the Jamaican society in order to survive.

The process of assimilation / integration of immigrant groups increased as younger generations all attended the same educational

Map 2: Lands of origin of Jamaicans

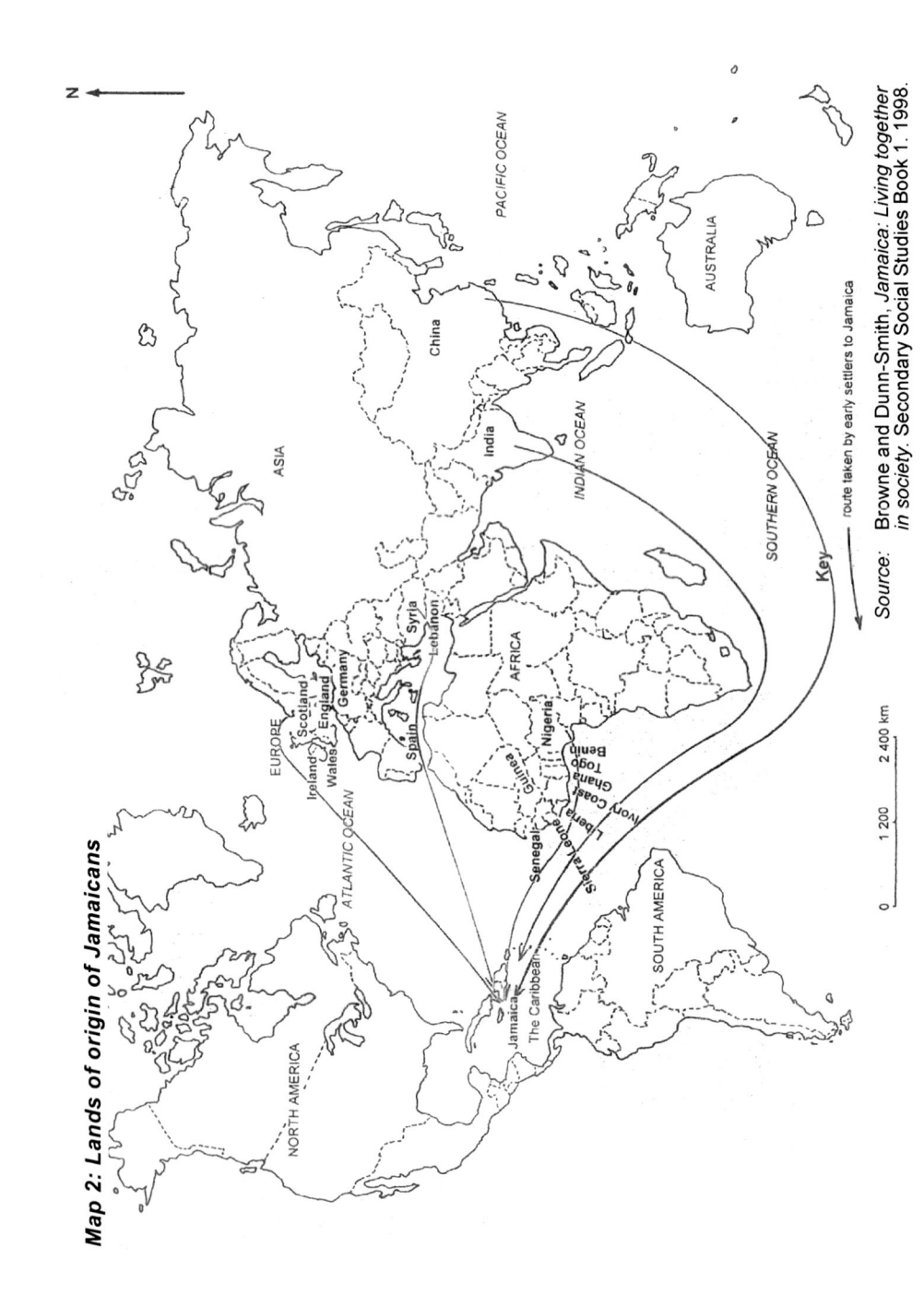

Source: Browne and Dunn-Smith, *Jamaica: Living together in society.* Secondary Social Studies Book 1. 1998.

institutions. Integration was further achieved by Christian groups which encouraged the immigrants to abandon the religion of their ancestors and become converts to one of the Christian denominations.

However, there are still groups of Africans, Jews, Lebanese, Chinese, Indians and Europeans who seek to preserve aspects of their traditional cultures. Some descendants of immigrants make trips to the homelands of their ancestors as a way of discovering and maintaining their roots.

This section aims to give a brief outline of each ethnic group, stating who they were, where they came from, their places of settlement, and their integration into the society. Special reference is made to family life.

3.1 Ethnic Groups Who Came

Tainos

Many of us learned that the name of the original inhabitanbts of Jamaica was "Arawak". Researchers now believe that Arawak is the name of a language that was spoken by many tribes in the Caribbean region, and that the Tainos were one such tribe. It is therefore considered that "Tainos" is the correct name of the earliest settlers who came to Jamaica from the Americas. Most of them died out during the Spanish occupation; a few remaining ones joined the Maroons. They are no longer identifiable as a surviving ethnic group in Jamaica.

Europeans

The Spanish, English, Scots, Welsh, Irish, German, Portuguese and French were the main European nationals who settled in the island.

It should be noted that some persons of British ancestry came from other parts of the British Empire. Europeans came as soldiers, naval and army officers, estate owners, estate overseers, bookkeepers, traders, merchants, missionaries, indentured workers, civil servants, doctors. The family history researcher will find much information on the European nationalities. There are many sources and leads to follow. Arrival dates of early European groups in the island are shown in Table 3.1.

Table 3.1: Arrival dates of some early European settlers

Ethnic Group	Date	Country of Origin	Where Settled
British	1655	United Kingdom, Barbados	Throughout the island
English	1656	Nevis and St. Kitts	Port Morant area, St. Thomas
English	1664	Barbados	No information
English	1675	Surinam (Jews?) with slaves	Surinam Quarters
English (Society of Friends)	1679	England	Parts of St. Elizabeth and Westmoreland, Spanish Town and Kingston
French	1803	Haiti	Various parts of the island
Jews	1494	Spain and Portugal via England, France, Holland, Germany	Throughout the island
Scots	1689	Darien, Panama	Parts of Westmoreland and St. Elizabeth
Spanish	1494	Spain	Throughout the island

Areas of settlement

Europeans lived primarily in coastal towns, in fertile valleys, on low hills, often on sites originally chosen by the Tainos. The wealthy owned sugar plantations and over time, built their impressive great houses. The less wealthy lived in small houses provided by the plantation owners, and in the towns and cities. Merchants built large elegant houses in the leading port towns. Many Europeans, who came as contract workers to estates after Emancipation, settled at higher elevations such as Brown's Town (the Irish) and Clarke's Town in St. Ann, Seaford Town (German) in Westmoreland with the greatest concentration between 1881 and 1921 being in Kingston.

The Jews

Jews from Europe have a long history of settlement in the island. Many came from Spain and Portugal during Spanish colonial rule in order to escape from religious persecution by Christians. Despite some of their difficulties in living under English colonial rule, many chose to remain in the island in order to enjoy the freedom of religion allowed here. The English restricted their activities to trading. After their businesses were destroyed by earthquake in 1692, they were granted the right to own land. They gained full political rights in 1831 and became politically active; by 1865 thirteen members of the House of Assembly were Jews and Jewish holidays were official holidays in the island.

Research Trails

Research trails are intended to lead the family historians to relevant sources pertaining to each ethnic group.

British trails

Records of European landowners including landholding maps showing family names for sugar estates, pimento and coffee walks and livestock pens.

German trails

Arrival dates of some indentured Germans (see page 106). German Museum and Sacred Heart Catholic Church, Seaford Town, Westmoreland.

Note: Many persons of German ancestry have emigrated to Canada and the United States of America.

Jewish trails

Jamaica Jewish Genealogical Society (see page 50), Jewish cemeteries (see page 30).

✡ Jewish Community Synagogue
    92 Duke Street, Kingston, Jamaica, West Indies
    (operated by the United Congregation of Israelites)

European References

English

Craton, Michael with the assistance of Garry Greenland, *Searching for the Invisible Man: Slaves and Plantation Life in Jamaica*, Harvard University Press, Cambridge, Mass. 1978. (Included in this book is the genealogy of several slave,coloured and white families from the records of Worthy Park Estate, Lluidas Vale, St. Catherine (then in St. John's parish). Sources used include slave and apprentice lists for 1730 and 1784-1838 and labourers' wage lists for 1840-1846, slave lists from the Registrar General's Department and church records (St. John's Parish Church).)

Higman, B.W., *Jamaica Surveyed – Plantation Maps and Plans of Eighteenth and Nineteenth Centuries*. Institute of Jamaica Publications Ltd. 1988

Scottish

My Church: The United Church in Jamaica and the Cayman Islands 2001, an historical survey that chronicles streams from which Presbyterian missionaries came and areas in which they lived and worked.

Irish

Mullally, Robert, 'The Irish in Jamaica' (excerpts of a speech given at the St. Patrick's Day Celebration 'Drowning the Shamrock' at the Wyndham Kingston Hotel) *The Jamaica Herald*, magazine supplement 'Pure Class', April 20, 1997

Senior, Carl, 'The Robert Kerr Emigrants: Irish Slaves for Jamaica' in Jamaica Journal #42. Institute of Jamaica Publications Ltd. 1978

Tortello, Rebecca, Dr., The arrival of the Irish in Jamaica. Out of many one culture. The People Who Came. *The Gleaner*, December 1, 2003

Williams, Father J.J., *Whence the Black Irish of Jamaica*, MacVeagh, New York, 1932

Jews

Andrade, Jacob A.P.M. *A Record of the Jews in Jamaica from the English Conquest to the Present Times*. The *Jamaica Times* Ltd., 8-12 King Street, Kingston, Jamaica, British West Indies, 1941

Delevante, Marilyn and Anthony Alberga, *An Account of the History of the Jews in Jamaica*. Ian Randle Publishers, 2005

DePass-Scott, Rosemarie, 'Spanish and Portuguese Jews of Jamaica'. *Jamaica Journal* #43. Institute of Jamaica Publications Ltd., 1979

'History of Jewish Congregations in Jamaica'. In the *Sunday Gleaner*, October 7, 2001, page F6. Sources: Prayer Book, United Congregation of Israelites & Jamaican Historical Structures and 'Shaare Shalom – the Gates of Peace' in *Jamaica Journal*, Institute of Jamaica Publications Ltd.

Mordecai, Arbell, *Portuguese Jews of Jamaica*, University of the West Indies Press, 2000

Silverman, Henry P., *The Tercentenary of the Official Founding of the Jewish Community of Jamaica*, Kingston, 1955

French

Bryan, Patrick, 'Emigres, Conflict and Reconciliation: The French Emigres in Nineteenth Century Jamaica'. *Jamaica Journal*, September 1973 Vol 7 No. 3. Institute of Jamaica Publications Ltd.

Germans

Fremmer, Ray, 'The People of Seaford Town'. *The Jamaican*, No. 2, 1988 Vol.11. A Rayne Publication

Seaford Town advertising feature. *The Gleaner* August 14, 2003

Senior, C.H., 'German Immigrants in Jamaica 1934-1938'. *Journal of Caribbean History* 10 and 11, 1978. Caribbean Press, St. Lawrence, Barbados

Muller, Elizabeth, 'Some Remnants of German Heritage in Jamaican Speech'. *Jamaica Journal* #45, Institute of Jamaica Publications Ltd. 1981

Africans

The first Africans were brought by the Spanish under licence from the Spanish Crown in 1523 to a French Governor, Laurent de Gorrewood. The number of Africans decreased up to 1655 since the Spanish colonists could not afford to buy them.

Under the English, however, the trade expanded. Africans came primarily from countries we now know as Nigeria, Ghana, Liberia and Niger. They were mainly from the Yoruba and Ibo ethnic groups of Nigeria and the Ashanti, Mandingo and Coromantee groups of Ghana. The majority worked on the sugar plantations.

Others worked at jobs associated with town life such as blacksmiths, higglers, tailors and sailors.

On the plantations, two categories of estate slaves can be identified:

- field slaves, drivers, artisans or skilled slaves, and those responsible for the boiling of the sugar – critical to the success and fortunes of the estate
- domestic or house slaves

Areas of settlement

Slaves were purchased by estates and taken to various parts of the island where their owners had their plantations. Some remained in the coastal towns as 'job slaves'.

Post-emancipation free villages

Landless, homeless, jobless and illiterate, thousands of Jamaicans of African descent started a new life in 1838 with freedom from slavery as their prized possession. Only a few had already purchased small lots of land in the free villages.

Did your ancestors live in a free village? If it was set up by a religious denomination, this may give you a clue for your family research since it is likely that your ancestor belonged to the denomination that established the free village. You may also find your family name on a map of the original estate that shows the subdivisions. Men and women became landowners of plots in the free villages. Table 3.2 shows how the number of lots under 10 acres grew between 1840 and 1865.

Table 3.2: Increase in number of lots under 10 acres, 1840-1865

Year	No. of lots under 10 acres
1840	883
1845	20,724
1865	60,000

Philip Sherlock and Hazel Bennett in 'The Story of the Jamaican People' (page 242) state that eventually about 2000 such villages were established. Establishment began in the then parishes of St. Andrew, St. John, Manchester and Metcalfe. According to the same authors (page 241) in 1845 there were 23 villages in Trelawny, 10 in St. Thomas-in-the-Vale and 10 in St. James. See Table 3.3.

Table 3.3: Locations and origins of some free villages

Name & Year established	Location	Founder and Denomination	Additional Information
Bethel Town Aug. 1, 1838	Near Rio Bueno, Trelawny	Rev. Thomas Burchell, Baptist	
Birmingham August, 1838	Near Falmouth, Trelawny	Rev. William Knibb, Baptist	
Buxton Town	St. Ann	Rev. John Clark, Baptist	Named for Thomas Fowel Buxton, an abolitionist, with funds from philanthropist Joseph Sturge
Clarksonville after Aug.1, 1838	Near Cave Valley, St. Ann	Rev. John Clark, Baptist	
Dumbarton	Dry Harbour Mtn., St. Ann		60 quarter-acre lots
Epworth	St. Ann	Methodist	
Goodwill, shortly before 1840	St. James	Rev. George Blythe, Presbyterian	Originally 15 acres of land divided into quarter-acre lots. The land was purchased for 900 pound which was collected by the congregation.
Granville	St. James	Rev. William Knibb, Baptist	Settlement of 90 acres named after Granville Sharp, an abolitionist, and founder of Sierra Leone
Harmony Hall 1838	Near Brown's Town, St. Ann	Rev. John Clark, Baptist	
Kettering	Near Falmouth, Trelawny	Rev. William Knibb, Baptist	

Name & Year established	Location	Founder and Denomination	Additional Information
Maldon Aug 1, 1838	St. Elizabeth	Rev. Walter Denby, Baptist	
Porus (Originally Vale Lionel)	Manchester	Rev. James Philippo, Baptist	Land presented to ex-slaves to build houses. Property was purchased by philanthropists and Baptist missionaries of Maldon, Essex, England. A land speculator, Andrew Drummond bought and subdivided 700 acres
Refuge	10 miles from Falmouth, Trelawny	Rev. William Knibb, Baptist	First called Wilberforce after the English abolitionist
Retreat Pen	Near Manchioneal, Portland		41 half-acre (more or less) lots
Sligoville officially opened June 12, 1840	St. Catherine	Rev. James Philippo, Baptist	25 acres divided into one and two acre lots; later increased to 50 acres. This was a planned settlement. The first lot was purchased by ex-slave, Henry Lurian. Completed township consisted of about 200 families. The 80-90 original owners of about one-acre lots paid seven pounds for the lot.
Sturge Town, 1839	St. Ann	Rev. John Clark – Baptist and Quakers (Society of Friends)	The town was named after Joseph Sturge – a Quaker philanthropist who visited Jamaica. Most of the money was contributed by the congregation. Sturge Town was original property part of Mt. Abylah property.
Trysee	Near Brown's Town, St. Ann		

Name & Year established	Location	Founder and Denomination	Additional Information
Sturge Town	St. Catherine	Rev. James Philippo, Baptist	Second free village established by Rev. Philippo. The original site was part of a 1000-acre estate which was later purchased in its entirety. Funds for the original purchase came from England.
Maidstone (also called Nazareth), 1840	Manchester	Moravian	Originally, this was a coffee plantation of 340 acres. It was divided into 98 lots varying from 1 to 15 acres in size.

Free Africans

The Maroons

The Maroons were originally slaves freed by the Spanish during the confiict with the English. The Spanish Maroons had come originally from western and Sub-Saharan areas of Africa. A 1999 study by historian Shana Afroz of the University of the West Indies, explored the Moorish, Islamic (Muslim) heritage of these Maroons.

Under English colonial rule, run-away African slaves joined the original Maroons in settlements located in remote hills in the interior of the island (see Map 3). Maroons have a strong oral tradition. They are proud of their long defiance of slavery, and of their rights and freedoms gained from the English. Maroons still enjoy some of these privileges in independent Jamaica.

Post-emancipation indentured Africans

Most Africans came as indentured workers 1840 to 1865 to work on sugar estates. After the slave trade ended in the British Empire (1807), a number of Africans destined to be slaves who were found on foreign ships, were set free by the British. Some were carried directly to the island, some to St. Helena. Some of those who

Researching Your Jamaican Family

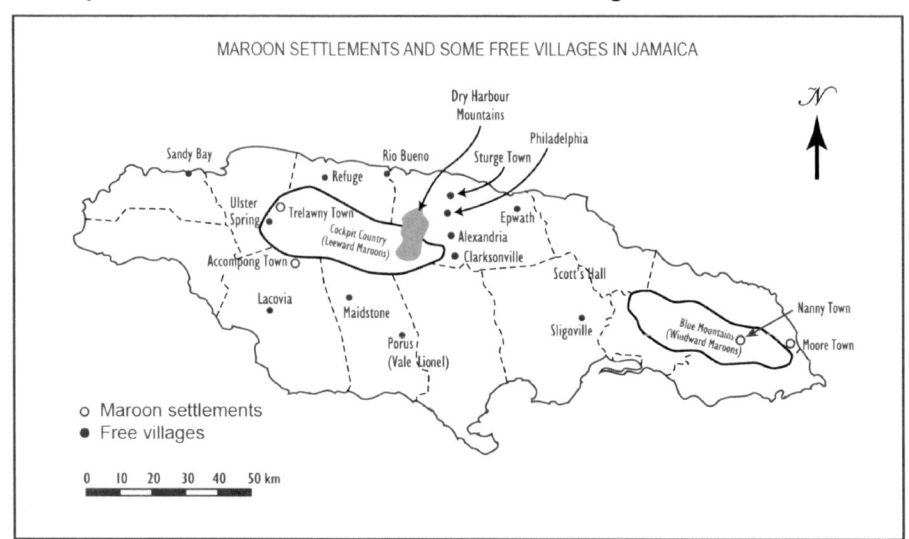

Map 3: Maroon settlements and some free villages in Jamaica

Source: Sherlock and Bennett, *The Story of the Jamaican People* (Kingston: Ian Randle Publishers Ltd. in collaboration with Kingston: Creative Production and Training Centre Ltd. (CPTC), 1988), p.136.

came were descendants of Maroons who had been expelled from Jamaica to Nova Scotia, Canada and then resettled in Sierra Leone.

Like all voluntary indentured workers, the contract of free Africans included a passage back to their homeland. Since this part of the arrangement did not work well, few were willing to come. Some of those who came ran away from the estates and easily blended into the society. Some left the estates at the end of their indenture and refused to re-indenture.

Indentured Africans arrived at a number of ports on the island and went to work in various parts of the country. Table 3.4 shows some of their areas of settlement.

Table 3.4: Some areas of settlement of voluntary indentured Africans

Parish	Location	Additional Information
Hanover	Lethe, Copse, Content, Chester Castle, Argyle, Plum Pen	A group of 85 boys, all under the age of 14, were sent to these areas from a government school in Sierra Leone. School and church attendance arrangements were made for them in Jamaica.
Hanover	Jericho	Etu people
St. Thomas	Estates in the Plantain Garden River Valley	Some estates on which they worked include Amity Hall (Sierra Leone workers), Rhine (Congolese people). It is said that most free Africans settled in this parish.

With only about 8000 indentured Africans coming, government turned to India for indentured workers for the estates.

African Ancestry from the West Indies and the United States of America

There was limited movement of people of African ancestry between the islands of the British West Indies. Some persons came with their European owners. Examples include persons who came from French Haiti, West Indies, at the time of the Haitian Revolution in 1791.

A few came with their owners from the United States of America at the time of the American War of Independence, 1775-1782. Their owners were Loyalists opposed to independence from England. Leile and Baker were two of these. They started the Native Baptist Church in 1782.

Research trails

African trails

Only a few persons may be able to trace their African slave ancestry in written records before 1817, but there are exceptions.

To garner information on African ancestry, the family historian has to seek for information in documents and materials prepared by Europeans. These sources include:

- ⚜ Wills of slave owners

- Slave return lists
- Deeds
- Manumission records
- Estate maps
- Inventory of properties
- Family letters of slave owners
- Birth, baptismal and death records

African References

Brathwaite, Edward Kamau, *The Development of Creole Society in Jamaica 1770-1820*, (new edition) Ian Randle Publishers, Kingston, Jamaica, West Indies. 2005. e-mail: irpl@colis.com.

Braithwaite, Edward Kamau, 'Maroon and Marooned' – a review of *The Maroons of Jamaica 1655-1796: A History of Resistance, Collaboration and Betrayal* by Mavis Grandby Campbell Bergin & Garvey, Mass. 1988

Carey, Beverley, *The Maroon Story*, Agouti Press, Jamaica 1997.

Craton, Michael, with the assistance of Garry Greenland, *Searching for the Invisible Man: Slaves and Plantation Life in Jamaica*. Harvard University Press, 1978.

Eubanks-Green, Lloyd, 'Roots of Islam: The Maroon Connection'. *The Gleaner*, Outlook, December 10, 2000 (p.13).

Higman, B. W., *Jamaica Surveyed: Plantation Maps of the 18th and 19th Centuries*, Institute of Jamaica Publications Ltd. 1988

Newton, Velma, *The Silver Men: West Indian Labour Migration to Panama, 1850-1914*. University of the West Indies Press, 1984.

Robinson, Carey, 'The Maroons – Masters of their own destiny'. *Skywritings* No. 89. October/November 1993. Creative Commications Inc. Ltd.

Senior, Olive, *A-Z of Jamaican Heritage*, Heinemann Educational Books (Caribbean) Ltd and The Gleaner Company Ltd, 1983. See 'African Heritage', 'Maroons', 'Free Africans'.

Post-emancipation indentured Africans

Jacobs, H. P., 'The Last Africans' – a review article in *Jamaica Journal* Vol.8 No.4, 1974. Institute of Jamaica Publications Ltd.

Schuler, Monica, *Alas! Alas ! Kongo. A Social History of Indentured African Immigration into Jamaica, 1841-1865*. Baltimore and London. John's Hopkins University Press 1980

Thomas, Mary Elizabeth, *Jamaica and Voluntary Laborers from Africa, 1840-1865*, Gainsville University Press of Florida, 1974

East Indians

Indentured Workers

Indentured Indian migration took place between 1845 and 1916. The first set landed at Old Harbour Bay on May 10, 1845. Of the total of 4551 who came before 1848, 1463 and their 263 children born in Jamaica went back to India. In a known case, one man who returned to India came back to live. Of those remaining, 1491 and their 92 children born in the island settled here; 500 went to Panama. Others died of cholera or other causes. The distribution of East Indians who worked on estates is shown on Map 4.

Independent Indians

Independent Indian migration began in the late nineteenth century. Many of these persons were merchants, sometimes being referred to as 'Bombay Indians'. Twentieth century immigrants include professionals – doctors, accountants, academics. Some return regularly to visit their homeland. Some independent immigrants are transitory, spending a number of years in the island and later migrating to the United States of America. Some independent migrants come from other parts of the Caribbean – Guyana and Trinidad. The group of wealthy independent Indians settled mainly in Kingston, Montego Bay and Ocho Rios.

Indian trails

- National Council for Indian Culture in Jamaica, Kingston.
- Arrival dates of some Indians 1845-1914 (see Table 4.9, p. 108).

Map 4: Location of some of the estates employing Indian immigrants 1879-1921

MAP OF JAMAICA SHOWING SOME OF THE ESTATES EMPLOYING INDIAN IMMIGRANTS, 1879-1921

Key

CLARENDON
(1) Whitney
(2) Retreat
(3) Denbigh
(4) Morelands
(5) Monymusk
(6) Amity Hall
(7) Bog
(8) Danks

HANOVER
(1) Old Retrieve
(2) New Retrieve

PORTLAND
(1) Windsor Castle
(2) Paradise
(3) Shrewbury
(4) Burlington
(5) Fellowship
(6) Tom's Hope
(7) Hopewell
(8) Williamsfield

ST. ELIZABETH
(1) Ipswich
(2) Holland

ST. THOMAS
(1) Amity Hall
(2) Hordley
(3) Golden Grove
(4) Duckenfield
(5) Philipsfield
(6) Potosi
(7) Lyssons
(8) Belvedere
(9) Albion

ST. JAMES
(1) Rose Hall
(2) Cinnamon Hill
(3) Latium
(4) Providence
(5) Seven Rivers
(6) Mocho

ST. CATHERINE
(1) Worthy Park
(2) Riversdale
(3) Harkers Hall
(4) Bushy Park

ST MARY
(1) Brimmer Hall
(2) Trinity
(3) Quebec
(4) Fontabelle
(5) Ballards Valley
(6) Llonrumney
(7) Orange Hill
(8) Green Castle
(9) Water Valley
(10) Clermont
(11) Montrose
(12) Newry
(13) Grays Inn
(14) Chovey
(15) Clonmel
(16) Fort George
(17) Fort Stewart

WESTMORELAND
(1) Pool Island
(2) Masemure
(3) Bellisle
(4) Frome
(5) Friendship
(6) Blackheath

Source: Verene Shepherd, *Transient to Settlers – The Experiences of Indians in Jamaica 1845-1950* (Centre of Research in Asian Immigration, the University of Warwick & Peepal Tree Books, 1994), p.38, fig.2.

Indian References

Mansingh, Laxmi and Ajai, *Home Away from Home – 150 years of Indian Presence in Jamaica 1845-1995*. Ian Randle Publishers, 1999

Mansingh, Laxmi and Ajai, 'The Indian Tradition Lives on'. *Skywritings* No. 89.October/November 1993.Creative Communications Inc. Ltd.

Shepherd, Verene, *Transients to Settlers – The Experiences of Indians in Jamaica 1845-1950*. Centre of Research in Asian Immigration, the University of Warwick & Peepal Tree Books, 1994.

Chinese

Indentured workers

The first Chinese indentured workers (267), mainly from Southern China, arrived in 1854, from Hong Kong. A further 205 came from Panama. Another group of 608 arrived July12, 1884. They also came from Southern China an area which was both hilly and rocky and subject to droughts and floods. The land was barely able to sustain the farming families who lived there. Each man agreed to work for seven years in return for a paid passage.

As with other immigrant groups, there were always more men than women. For example, of a group who came in 1884, there were 508 males, 109 females, 17 girls and 3 infants. Family groups were kept intact under an Immigration Law of 1879 which stated that:

> In making allotments, husbands shall not be separated from their wives, nor minors and infants from their parents or natural guardians, and so far as possible, members of the same family, neighbours from the same village or persons who agree in representing themselves to be friends and associates should not be separated from each other.

Source: The Laws of Jamaica – Law 23 of 1879

After indentureship, many Chinese became shopkeepers and their shops became common in many Jamaican towns and villages. Throughout the years, Chinese merchants have held a place in retail and wholesale businesses and in the financial sector of the island. Some Chinese are now in other professional fields, e.g. medicine and architecture. Many Chinese became Roman Catholics.

In 1920, Chinese immigrants numbered close to 4000. By 1930 the census showed that there were 6,500 Chinese in the island. In 1947 an annual quota of 20 with wives and children was set. In 1956 an additional 20 per year were allowed in order to bring in dependent parents.

Independent immigrants

Since indentureship ended, many independent Chinese immigrants have continued to come to Jamaica in smaller numbers – many to join family members. Chinese immigrants include persons from Hong Kong and mainland China. Hong Kong was a British colony until 1999 when it reverted to being a part of mainland China.

Areas of settlement

The Chinese community is scattered throughout the island, with the greatest number in Kingston and St. Andrew. Indentured workers were sent to the following parishes:

- Clarendon
- Portland
- St. Andrew – Constant Spring estate
- St. Catherine – Caymanas estate
- St. Mary
- St. Thomas in the East – Plantain Garden area, Lyssons and Coley estates
- Westmoreland – Blue Castle and Myersfield estates

Chinese trails

Old letters, address books, name of markets in ancestors' home towns and reasons for their departure.

- Arrival dates of some Chinese 1854-1888 (see Table 4.8, p. 108)
- Chinese Cultural Association, 22 Barbican Road, Kingston 6, Jamaica, West Indies
- Chinese Benevolent Association Ltd. 129 Barry Street, Kingston, and 176 Old Hope Road, Kingston 6, Jamaica, West Indies
- World Hakka Conference (Hakka means 'guest people').
- Chinese Cemetery, Waltham Park Road, St. Andrew, Jamaica, West Indies. Officially opened 1911.
- Chinese migration to Canada and the United States of America, many going in the 1970s.

Chinese References

Barrett, Michelle, 'Chinese tales etched in stone'. *The Gleaner*, January 31, 2004. Section C. Page C1

Chen, Ray, The Shopkeepers – Commemorating 150 years of the Chinese in Jamaica. Periwinkle Publishers

Chen, Julie, The Chinese in Jamaica – 150 Years of Nation Building:1854–2004, Celebrating Chinese New Year, January 22, 2004. The Year of the Monkey. A Gleaner Supplement.

Chinsee, Helen, 'A Chinese in Jamaica', in *Jamaica Journal* Vol. 2 No. 1, March 1968. Institute of Jamaica Publications Ltd.

Lee, Tom Lin, *Jamaican Chinese Worldwide – One Family*. Huntsmill Graphics Ltd., Canada. 2004

Lee, Easton, *From Behind the Counter (Poems from a rural Jamaican experience)*. Ian Randle Publishers, 1988

Lee, Easton, *Heritage Call: Ballad for the Children of the Dragon*. Ian Randle Publishers, 2001

Levy, Jacqueline, 'The Economic Role of the Chinese in Jamaica: The Grocery Retail Trade', *Jamaica Historical Review* XV, 1986. Jamaica Historical Society

Levy, Jacqueline, 'Chinese Indentured Immigration to Jamaica during the Latter Part of the Nineteenth Century' – a paper presented at the Fourth Conference of Caribbean Historians, April 9–14, 1972

Lyew-Ayee, Parris A., 'Call me Mr. Chin' in Celebrating Chinese New Year, January 22, 2004. The Year of the Monkey. A Gleaner Supplement

Senior, Olive, 'The Panama Railway: The Chinese Who came from Panama' in *Jamaica Journal* #44. Institute of Jamaica Publications Ltd.

Tortello, Rebecca. The Arrival of the Chinese. *Jamaica Gleaner*: Pieces of the Past, Sept. 1, 2003. http://www.jamaicagleaner.com/pages/history

Middle Eastern Ancestry – Lebanese (Syrian)

Most ancestors of these Jamaicans came first from Lebanon, others from Damascus and Bethlehem, all of which were a part of the country then called Syria. Today, Damascus is in present day Syria. Bethlehem is in Palestine and Lebanon is a separate country.

Originally, the Lebanese were Greek Orthodox Christians or Jews. Many of the first Lebanese who were Greek Orthodox Christians became Anglicans. Many immigrants from Bethlehem and Syria became Roman Catholics.

The first Lebanese came in 1891 to the great International Exhibition. Many of those who came for the exhibition sent for their families. Like those who followed, many of the first Lebanese were traders in clothing and dry goods. Many travelled, often walking throughout the country, crediting or 'trusting' goods to customers and collecting their money on their return.

Many Lebanese are at the centre of retail, wholesale, industrial, professional, financial and tourism activities in the island.

Lebanese (Syrian) trails

- Arrival dates of Lebanese
- Anglican and Roman Catholic records of births, marriages and deaths

Lebanese References

Ammar, Nellie, 'They Came from the Middle East'. *Jamaica Journal* Vol. 4 No. 1, March 1970. Institute of Jamaica Publications Ltd.

Nicholls, David, 'The "Syrians" of Jamaica'. *Historical Review* XV, pp.50-61, 1986. (Jamaica Historical Society).

3.2 Composition of Jamaica's Population

Government population censuses provide data on the island's ethnic groups. Table 3.5 shows Jamaica's population by native country in the 1861 Census, with the island's total population being 441,264.

*Ethnic Roots
of Jamaican Families*

Table 3.5: Jamaica's population by native country, Census 1861. Nationalities numbering 40 and over are shown.

Native country	Numbers in 1861	Native country	Numbers in 1861
Africa	10,501	Indies, West	253
America	282	Indies, West, British	99
Barbados	42	India	1, 541
Calcutta and Madras	51	Ireland	474
China	239	Jamaica*	423,071
Cuba	40	Madiera	179
Denmark	81	Portugal	163
England	1,856	Scotland	600
France	47	Spain	60
Germany	253	Spaniards	99
Hayti	206	Others	472
Indies, East	668		

* Persons born in Jamaica belonging to a number of ethnic groups.

Source: Census Summary, 1861

The 1861 Census also classified the population as follows:

White	Black	Brown	Total
13,816	343,374	81,065	441,264

Changes in the island's ethnic composition are shown in Table 3.6.

73

Table 3.6: Ethnic origin of Jamaica's population: 1982, 1991 and 2001

Ethnic origin	1982	1991	2001
Negro/Black	1,622,473	2,080,323	2,378,104
East Indian	29,283	29,218	23,227
Chinese	5,329	5,372	5,153
Syrian/Lebanese	759		
White	4,841	5,200	4,716
Mixed/Negro	278,015	Mixed 166,991	Mixed 161,234
Other Mixed	24,813		
Other races	1,206	1,252	Other 2,117
Not stated	206,169	11,317	Not reported 21,411
Total population	**2,172,879**	**2,299,673**	**2,595,962**

Sources: 2001 Population Census; *Jamaica and Statistical Yearbook of Jamaica, 1999*, STATIN 2000

3.3 Place Names as Clues to Ethnicity

Place names often give clues to the origin of the people who first lived in an area. This is useful information for the family historian.

The Spanish gave names to many places in the island. All those beginning with 'Rio' or 'Don' are Spanish names. A look at a map of Jamaica shows a good number of them which are still in use.

Most place names, however, have British origin – English, Scottish, Welsh, Irish. Owners of plantations and cattle pens named their properties after their family names or after places they came from. Parishes and counties were named after royalty, governors and biblical characters. Some missionaries (notably the Moravians and Presbyterians) chose place names from the Bible.

Table 3.7 gives some examples of the ethnic origins of the names of some towns, villages, districts, streets, lanes, geographical features.

While doing your research, look for place names associated with your family, as ancestors may be mentioned in the information. Look out for changes in some place names, as well as changes in the spelling of some place names. Several places in the island have the same name so note the parish in which the place being researched is located. Note too that print and photograph collections of specific places in the island are to be found in books, magazines and libraries.

Table 3.7: Ethnic origin of some Jamaican place names

Ethnic Origin	Place names
African	Accompong, Mocho, Abeokuta
English	Portland, Cornwall, Somerset, Kingston, Newmarket, Wakefield, Clarks Town, Chatham, Windsor Castle, Albion, Bath, Bowden, Falmouth, Oxford, Titchfield, Winchester
French	Montpelier, Pechon Street
German	Halberstaat, Hanover
Indian	Madras, Bengal
Irish	Dublin Castle, Bangor Ridge, Ulster Spring, Kildare, Middleton, Leinster Road, Kinsale Avenue, Antrim, Enfield
Jewish	Dias, Gaza
Scottish	Kintyre, Huntley, Moy Hall, Glasgow, Clydesdale, Kilmarnock, Deeside, Dundee, Tweedside, Dumfries, Moffat
Spanish	Rio Grande, Rio Cobre, Don Figuerrero, Pedro (Plains), Ocho Rios, Santa Cruz
Taino	Guanaboa, Liguanea
Welsh	Llandewey, Lloyds, Lluidas Vale, Denbigh, Pembroke

The *Dictionary of Place Names in Jamaica* by Inez Sibley (published by the Institute of Jamaica, Kingston, Jamaica 1978) sometimes includes information on persons associated with some place names.

In all societies changes constantly occur. You will find changes in the appearance and character of a settlement – district, village, town or city. I had the disappointing experience of going to look for an elderly lady in an old house, only to find the lot occupied by a multi-storey office block!

3.4 Family Names as Clues to Ethnicity

Your own last name (surname / family name) and those of your relatives and friends are very much the result of history.

Some of the ethnic groups who came had traditional ways of naming their children. As each group became integrated into Jamaican society, they adopted the norm of the country. This is the English norm in which women take the surnames of their husbands and in which children of the marriage use their fathers' surnames. It is also the norm for each person to have a Christian or first name and usually one or more middle names.

Some non-British families completely changed their names – first and last. For example, the name Williams is one used by people of Chinese, African and Indian descent. In the earlier years of their arrival, many of the Chinese retained their custom of having the family/surname first. However over time, they changed to the British custom of having the surname last. It should be noted that some non-British families changed their names when they were baptized into the Christian religion; they took Christian (British) names.

During slavery children born to African women of non-African fathers sometimes acquired the surname of their fathers. Non-African fathers included estate owners, estate managers, bookkeepers. Some Africans changed from one British name to another when they were manumitted.

After Emancipation, ex-slaves and some Maroons also followed this practice. Sometimes the ex-slaves used the names of people they had worked for. A true story known to the writer is that of one Post-Emancipation grandfather who gave all his children a different surname, as he did not like his own. Challenge for the family historian!

After Emancipation, many children born out of wedlock were given their mothers' surnames. Among some social groups children of young girls were given the girls' family names so that mother and daughter had the same surname. Often, the community regarded them as siblings. This is therefore something you need to investigate very tactfully.

The official registration of births began on April 1, 1878. Prior to that date christening/baptism records or recording in family Bibles are the most likely sources of information. Jamaican Anglican Church Parish Registers date from the 1660s to 1880s.

Up to 1981 the name of a child's father could only be recorded on the birth certificate if the father was present at the time of registration. In that year the law changed and a father's name could be entered without his actual presence. Since then the law allows the late addition of a father's name to a child's birth certificate.

Table 3.8 shows some names associated with ethnicity and countries of origin.

Table 3.8: Ethnic origin of some Jamaican surnames

Ethnic Origin	Surnames
Chinese	Chang, Chin, Chue, Chung, Fung, HoSang, Kong, Lee, Lue, Lyn, Lue-Lim, Lyn-Fatt, Sang, Tai, Wong, Yap-Sang, Ying
English	Blake, Brown, Dickenson, Knibb, Noble, Norris, Pinnock, Richardson, Smith, Tinson, Willis, Willmott
German	Hacker, Hahn, Helwig, Lanaman, Manhertz, Schloss, Stiebel
Indian	Beckaroo, Ballysingh, Cheddisingh, Chutkan, Dadlani, Lakasingh, Maragh, Parboosingh, Ramcharan, Ramjeet, Sirjue, Varma
Irish	Browne, Collin, Eubanks, Manigan, McCormack, O'Connor, O'Meally, O'Sullivan, Walch
Jewish	Alvarenga, Bravo, Cohan, DaCosta, DeCordova, DeLisser, Fernandez, Gabay, Hart, Israel, Lindo, Lopez, Nunes, Pinto, Rodriques, Senior, Tavares, Vaz,
Lebanese	Ammar, Azan, Hanna, Issa, Josephs, Khaleel, Matalon, Shoucair
Scottish	Gordon, McDonald, McKenzie, Murray, Robertson, Stuart

Names of African Ancestry before Emancipation – Trails

- Court records, deeds and inventories
- Family letters of slave owners
- Records of European landowners in, for example, Barry Higman's *Jamaica Surveyed: Plantation Maps and Plans of the 18th and 19th Centuries*, Institute of Jamaica Publications Ltd. 1988. Some maps and plans give information on names, ethnicity, mothers' names, sex, age.

- Slave return lists from 1817–1832 required by law from slave owners every three years. Lists show names (the majority with surnames), ages, sex, colour, African or Creole (ethnicity) of each slave. The Jamaica Archives and Records Office has these lists filed by parishes.
- Church records – Jamaican Church of England (Anglican) Parish Records of births, marriages and deaths of coloureds indicate persons who were coloured. After Emancipation baptismal and marriage records show ex-slaves with surnames. Between 1834 and 1838, on being baptized and/or married, some apprentices changed their names.
- Non-Anglican records contain names and information about free coloureds. In *Coke, the Man and his Mission: The Church in Early Years* by John Poxon, there is a reference (p. 70) to James Taylor, a Coke (Methodist) Local Preacher, who sought to have marriages performed by non-Anglican ministers before Emancipation legally recognized after Emancipation. The Act was entitled 'An Act to Legalize, Register and Confirm Marriages by Dissenters and other Ministers not connected with the Established Church' (the Anglican Church).
- Wills of slave owners may show names of those manumitted (that is, slaves granted their freedom). Manumission lists 1734–1838 are available at the Jamaica Archives and Records Office.

3.5 Family Life in Jamaica

Family life of all ethnic groups was severely disrupted in Jamaica. Immigration statistics from the early days of Spanish colonization show that the ratio of women to men was always low; there were always more male immigrants than female immigrants. This situation was resolved in different ways.

European

Among Europeans, the nuclear family with father, mother and children was the socially accepted norm. Couples were legally married with the blessing of the Anglican Church.

Some men married British women, but because they were few in number in the island, bachelors sometimes went 'back home' to find wives. It is interesting to note that widows did not remain widows for long! Some men never married and some spent some time in the island before marrying. These two groups selected partners from among African women. These unions gave rise to the coloured (brown) population of the island. Unmarried people living together were described as 'living common-law'. Their children were described as illegitimate (unlawful) or as bastards. The mothers and children did not have the same rights as legal wives and legal children.

Visiting unions in which men and women established sexual relations without living under the same roof, was another type of union that developed.

African

As a result of the way the slave trade operated, African families were likely to be split apart in Africa and also on arrival in Jamaica. The slaves lived in 'slave villages' on the plantations – each village being made up of several huts. The slaves and their children were regarded as property of their owners. Mothers were expected to care their babies, but families could be broken up and sold if the owner wished. This situation remained so until a law was passed forbidding the arbitrary break-up of families. This law indicates that there were well established family households among slaves.

The biological link between mother and baby was recognised, and perhaps the 'pickney'(field) gang that weeded under the supervision of the old women also provided opportunities for emotional bonding. In addition, there were the women who cooked for men, women and children.

It is possible that this has contributed to the largely matriarchal system among Jamaicans of African ancestry. The system of mother often being the head of the household has resulted in many children interacting mainly with their mother's family and with grandmothers often being the important focus of the family. This is so, especially when the grandmother has helped with the rearing of grand and even great-grandchildren.

Such extended families evolved as a pattern of family life. The older generation assisted the younger parents with child-rearing and household chores. In later life, the young in turn cared for the older folk.

Because the Anglican Church did not admit slaves, slave couples could not be legally married. When the influence of denominations other than Anglicans (dissenters/non-Anglicans) came to bear, ex-slaves were free to marry legally and with the blessing of the church. Persons of African descent began to enter official marriage relationships with the man as the head of the household. Eventually, the Anglican Church changed its policy and began to admit Africans to membership.

East Indian

East Indians came from a culture of joint family systems, in which a number of siblings with their nuclear families lived together in the same household or in the same yard. Estate management did not allow for this.

In India, men were heads of households and made major decisions, including selection of marriage partners, for their children. Usually marriages were arranged within religious groups – Hindu or Muslim. Up until 1895, Indians in the island, as far as possible, followed the marriage practices of their homeland. But in 1896, the Indian Immigrants Marriage, Divorce and Succession Law set the minimum age of marriage at 13 for girls and 15 for boys (Section 13 (1) of Law 22, 1896). A revision in 1929 – the Age of Marriage Act – increased the age of marriage to 16 for both sexes.

The law required that Hindu and Muslim couples acquire a 'Certificate of No Impediment' from the Protector of Immigrants. After the ceremony, the couple, along with the Hindu or Muslim priest who conducted the wedding and two witnesses, were required to go to Kingston within 48 hours to the Protector. The couples then signed the necessary documents to have the marriage legally recognized and recorded. The process proved cumbersome and resulted in many Hindu and Muslim unions not being recognized. This had a long term effect on the children of the traditional unions, as they were seen as 'bastards' under the law and had no legal right to inherit property. Indians who became Christians could be married by Christian Ministers, once they obtained the 'Certificate of No Impediment'.

In 1957 Hindu and Muslim priests were allowed to become marriage officers. The law was made retroactive to 1954.

Indian marriage partners are still preferred, but over the years the number of partners of other racial groups has increased. Many Indian young people now select their own partners.

Chinese

The Chinese also came from a tradition of extended family households.

Immigrant Chinese men faced the same problem of few women as European and Indian men did. For example, in the 1880s a group of 680 Chinese immigrants came from Hong Kong. Of that number 501 were men, 105 were women, 54 were boys and 17 were girls. In 1935 the government granted permission for 60 women to come from Hong Kong to help alleviate the problem.

Some men looked back to China and Hong Kong for spouses, but over time some have married outside of the ethnic group.

Following are some laws that affected Jamaican families after Emancipation

1878: A law was passed for the compulsory registration of births and deaths.

1879: A marriage law provided for the appointment of Marriage Officers (other than clergymen) so civil marriages could take place.

1880: Registration of marriages made compulsory.

1935, October 10: The Jamaican government granted permission for 60 'Chinese sweethearts' from the Far East to enter the island over the next three years. The intended husbands had to give a bond with two responsible sureties in the sum of 100 pounds. The young ladies had to be married within a specified time.

1969, May 21: The Attorney General announced the amendment of the Bastardy Act. It was changed to the Affiliation Law and the term 'bastard' was changed to 'natural child'.

1975, Dec. 18: The Family Court was established to deal specifically with family matters.

1976, August 5: The Status of Children Act was passed giving those born out of wedlock equal status to those born in wedlock in respect of inheritance. The law allowing paternity to be established by blood tests came into effect November 12, 1976.

1979, December 31: The Maternity Leave Law was passed. This law provided for eight weeks of leave with full pay and four weeks without pay for pregnant women over 18 years old.

1989: The Matrimonial Causes Act established no-fault divorce.

Burial of the dead

The death of a family member is always a significant event. Sometimes a death marks the end of a line or of one branch of a family. It is an occasion both of separation from the deceased and an opportunity for bonding between the remaining family members.

Europeans held burial services for their dead. Services were immediately followed by interment (burial) of the body. Burials took place in churchyards, at homes in family plots and in public cemeteries. The wealthy had elaborate tombstones with information about the deceased, sometimes including the cause of death.

The Jews had special cemeteries throughout the island, but their number has been gradually reduced (see page 30).

Many Jamaicans maintain a mixture of African and European customs. Many families keep wakes, nine-night, set-up, forty-night and a feast immediately after burial as part of their mourning expression.

Mourners sometimes seek to appease spirits in a number of ways. One example is the use of rum at the digging of graves.

Traditionally in India, Muslims bury their dead and Hindus cremate their dead on a pyre in public. Hindus then disposed of the ashes at sea or in the river, and in a few cases by burial. But cremation was not allowed at that time in Jamaica and so, the majority of Indians had no choice but to dispose of the dead by burial in the earth. Until the 1960s when cremation was introduced into the island, Indians who could afford it buried their dead at sea in lead coffins.

In 1911 a Chinese cemetery was officially opened in Kingston on lands developed in 1907. Prior to that, burials took place in church or public cemeteries. Today only a few Chinese use the cemetery; many being buried in church or public cemeteries.

Using Jamaican History in Family Research

To successfully undertake historical research beyond the time of your grandparents, it is recommended that you gain or review your knowledge and understanding of certain aspects of Jamaica's history.

The history of Jamaican families is bound up with several factors:

1. communication
2. defence, law and order
3. education and culture
4. freedom and civil rights
5. government
6. land ownership and inheritance
7. migration patterns
8. money
9. natural hazards
10. religion

We need to recognize that some events, while not of national importance, are significant in the life of individuals and their families. The material, therefore, highlights several relevant events for the years 1494-2004. These are well chronicled in historical publications, some of which are listed on page 116.

Development in the Arts, Sports and Culture are examples of areas of individual achievements that are not contained in the notes. Records of such accomplishments are available in newspapers, audio-visual sources and special publications.

Only a few natural hazards – hurricanes, floods, droughts, earthquakes – have been included. They impact the whole island – the landscape, economic and social life and they challenged affected families.

A complete list of all slave revolts, riots and other examples of challenges to the existing social order have been omitted in favour of the most significant ones.

The majority of the headings are divided into two historical periods – Pre-emancipation and Post-emancipation. The notes present more details on the Post-emancipation period, 1838-2004, as this is the period in which most Jamaicans of non-European ancestry will be able to trace their family histories. It is hoped that the information provided will enable you to place the history of your family in its historical context.

How to use the historical notes to assist your family research

The historical notes provide information about dates and events that will inform your research into the lives and activities of your ancestors. Here are some examples of how you can use the information:

- If your family is of East Indian origin from India, you will be able to find out when Indian nationals first came to the island. You will therefore be able to narrow your search to a date after 1845. (See 4.7 Migration Patterns.)
- Persons who know that a family member went to Panama to work will be able to find out when Jamaicans first migrated to Panama. (See 4.7 Migration Patterns.)
- Knowing the date when telephone service was first installed in the island will assist you to decide if a family member was listed in the telephone directory which you can consult. (See 4.1 Communication.)
- Persons who know that an ancestor went to high school after gaining a place in the Common Entrance Examination will be able to obtain the date when this examination was first used for selection of high school students. (See 4.3 Education and Culture.)

☙ Families whose ancestors had a religious connection will find information on the dates when the different religions and some Christian denominations established missions in the island and where those missions were established. (See 4.10 Religion.)

4.1 Communication

Family members use all available means of communication to keep in touch with each other – letters, telegrams, cablegrams, telephones, e-mail, cars, trucks, trains, ships, aeroplanes, the press. The content of written material is invaluable information for the family historian; it gives the researcher access to past events, concerns, personal matters and opinions. Available methods of transportation are clues to population movement. The systems needed to permit the use of these methods have been established in Jamaica over time.

Pre-emancipation

We know for certain that the Spanish built a road system that linked the capital, St. Jago de la Vega – to the main hatos (ranches) in the island. The English used and expanded the road system. In addition, they had a system of bonfires to signal the approach of enemy ships.

Sea captains carried correspondence and goods to and from the island for planters and merchants. It is more than likely that the Spanish did the same. However, changes were to come.

1663	The English King ordered the governor to establish a post office under the management of the Postmaster General of London. This was the first system to be set up in a British colony.
1670	Mail landed at Passage Fort was taken by road to St. Jago.
1671	Second post office was set up at Port Royal and a local Postmaster General was appointed. Planters and merchants had to go or send to Port Royal to collect their mail.

1711 'An Act for Establishing a General Post Office for all Her Majesty's Domains' under the Postmaster of London was passed. The act set the rates for overseas and local mail.

1720 Post Office established in Kingston under management of London Post Office.

1750 Organisation of internal postal service began.

1754 Thirty-four post offices across the island.

1763 Mail service from Falmouth to the United States of America (Pensicola and Charleston) started.

1830 Mail service to Haiti and Santo Domingo began.

1834 First issue of *The Gleaner* as a weekly publication.

Post-emancipation

1838 The Royal Mail Steam Packet Company (a private venture) was founded. The company carried all sea mail up to 1914.

The Jamaica Railway Corporation was established in November, the first railway to be built in a British colony. The rail line ran from Kingston to Angels (near Spanish Town). It provided work for some rural people and enabled easier transportation to and from rural areas.

1850 General Post Office established in Kingston with 42 other post offices linked by 5 post roads: Windward Road to Manchioneal; Northside Road to Port Antonio; Northside Road to Port Maria; Northside Road to Green Island; Leeward/Southside to Grange Hill.

1858-1860 First stamps – British – went on sale.

1859 Telegraph system started.

1860 Issue of Jamaican stamps began.

1869 The telegraph cable system to Europe (operated by the post office) was established.

July 1: Jamaica Railway Corporation extended its line to Old Harbour.

Using Jamaican History in Family Research

1875	A street car service (trams) was started in Kingston by a private company.
1879	Government bought the Jamaica Railway Corporation
1885	Railway line was extended from Old Harbour to Porus and Ewarton. Stations were established at May Pen, Four Paths and Clarendon Park.
1892	*April:* Jamaica Telephone Company formed.
1895	Railway line was extended to Montego Bay.
1896	Railway line to Port Antonio was built.
1900	Jamaica's first pictorial stamp was issued. It carried a picture of Llandovery Falls.
1901	The Imperial Direct Line, a private shipping line to England, was started. It helped the development of the banana trade by providing shipping to England.
1930	*December 2:* First commercial aircraft – a 'flying boat' flown by renowned aviator Charles Lindeberg landed on the sea at Harbour Head, Kingston. This was the beginning of an airmail postal service.
1936	A radio telephone link to the United States of America, England, Canada, Mexico and Cuba was established.
1939	*April 1:* Telephones were installed throughout the island. An all-island trunk connected the main towns.
1945	Palisadoes Airport opened to accomodate aeroplanes that replaced 'flying boats'.
1948	Jamaica Public Service abolished trams in favour of buses as public transport.
1950	*July:* The Jamaica Broadcasting Company (JBC) began broadcasting. In 1958 the company changed its name to Radio Jamaica and Rediffusion (RJR) – a private company.
1959	A second radio station – Jamaica Broadcasting Corporation (JBC) went on the air. The station was run by a statutory board of the government. An air terminal was opened in Montego Bay.
1963	JBC television began transmission.

1969	*April 1*: Air Jamaica Limited, the national airline, started operation.
1971	JAMINTEL – Jamaica International Communications Limited – started as a joint venture between the Government of Jamaica and Cable and Wireless.
1989	New radio stations – KLAS, Irie FM, Radio Waves started.
1992	Another newspaper, the *Jamaica Herald* started publication. It folded two years later.
1993	CVM-TV, LOVE FM (radio) and the *Observer* (newspaper) started operations.
2000	Information Technology Act allowed for an increase in the number of telecommunications providers and range of telecommunications services. Mobile telephones and internet services have increased contact between Jamaicans at home and those overseas.

4.2 Defence, Law & Order

The following information will assist researchers whose family members have served or still serve in the Jamaica Militia, the Police Force, the Jamaican Armed Forces, the West Indian Armed Forces, the British Armed Forces. It also provides information about the state of security throughout the island at different times giving the context in which families lived.

Pre-emancipation

The number of Spanish settlers was very small, so they kept a small army. This was no match for the English invaders in 1655. Many coastal towns and parish capitals on the coast still have remains of forts built by the British to guard the ports and the island against attacks by rival European countries.

From 1655 to the 1800s internal law and order was maintained by the professional army and a militia consisting of all white men. The militia was organized on a county and parish basis. Each county had a regiment of horse. Each parish had a muster ground where members of the militia met regularly for training in the use of arms.

The militia was subject to the orders of the governor who carried out regular inspections. When necessary, the militia was called on to quell riots or to defend the island. Militiamen were expected to provide their arms and horses.

1694   French forces attacked the north and east coasts of the island. The invasion lasted one month. The French were eventually repulsed by, it is said, 250 militiamen, but not before considerable damage had been done.

1728   The local militia got the aid of 2 regiments from Gibraltar (Europe), to protect planters and their estates against the Maroons.

1779   A regiment formed in North Carolina took the name the West India Regiment. It was made up of American Royalists opposed to the separation of that country from England. Many Loyalists left the United States of America to live in Royalist colonies like Canada, Jamaica and The Bahamas.

1832   An Act was passed to organize a police force to replace the militia and take over responsibility for law enforcement and public safety. Police were to be armed and equipped like the British army.

1833   Police ranks of Constable, Petty Constable and Watchmen were established.

Post-emancipation

1856   The ranks of Constable, Petty Constable and Watchmen were all combined. The all-male force consisted of 15 Inspectors, 41 Sergeants, 406 Constables. Inspectors took their orders from the governor.

1867   The Jamaica Constabulary Force was organized like the Royal Irish Constabulary. Recruits were trained in Spanish Town. A number of Irish men came as senior officers.

1906	The militia was officially disbanded. The St. Andrew Rifle Corp (a semiofficial body) was formed. It included members of the former militia.
1914	World War I started. The Jamaica Reserve Regiment was formed for the defence of the island.
1915	*November 8:* One contingent of Jamaican volunteers (consisting of some 500 men) went to join the British Armed Forces.
1916	Three more contingents (January 7, March 16, September 30) went to England.
1917	One other contingent went to England making a total of 10,000 Jamaican men in five contingents. For the first time women volunteers went to join the nursing service for the fighting forces.
1918	World War I ended.
1926	The West India Regiment was disbanded. They had their final parade at Up-Park-Camp. The Jamaica Military Band with their distinct Zouave uniforms is all that remains of that Regiment.
1939	World War II started. Many Jamaicans (members of the Jamaica Infantry Volunteers (JIV) went to join the armed forces in England.
1945	World War II ended. Some volunteers returned; some remained in England. The Jamaica Battalion was formed.
1948	Police Force was again reorganized in face of social changes and unrest. The post of Commissioner of Police was created.
1949	The first women (3) joined the police force.
1955	The Jamaica Regiment was formed.
1958	The Jamaica Regiment was disbanded and a West India Regiment was formed with men from the member countries of the West Indian Federation. This regiment absorbed men from the Jamaica Regiment.
1961	*February 27:* The Jamaica Territorial Regiment was formed.

Independence

1962   The Jamaica Defence Force (JDF) was formed after the West India Regiment was again disbanded.

4.3 Education and Culture

The history of many families includes the educational achievement of children, and of their subsequent jobs and professions. At first, in many families, parents could only afford to send some children to school (sometimes, only one), and that often at great sacrifice by themselves and the other siblings. As time went on opportunities widened and school became more accessible to a greater number of children.

Pre-emancipation

Nothing is known about the education of children between 1494 and 1655.

Under English colonial rule, private tutors and small private schools educated children of the wealthy. Parents who could afford it sent their children (mainly sons, white and sometimes, coloured) to schools in Europe. A few slaves learned to read and write; this was a special favour granted by liberal masters and/or as a result of the work of missionaries from England. The reading text was usually the Bible.

Up to 1813, Free Schools were only for poor whites. Commencing in 1814 free coloured children were allowed to attend Free Schools.

Table 4.1 highlights some of the Free Schools established in the island before Emancipation.

1829   Training for female teachers started by the Moravians at New Carmel Station, Westmoreland.

1834   Mico Charity founded with funds bequeathed by Lady Mico (of England) in 1670. Primary schools were established throughout the British West Indies. The Jamaica Mico School had a teacher training department.

1836   Opening of Mico College. This first teacher training college was also funded by the bequest from Lady Mico. The college was exclusively for teacher training.

Table 4.1: Pre-emancipation Free schools

Name	Parish	Year	Additional Information
Mannings	Westmoreland	1738	Bequest of Thomas William Manning
Rusea's	Hanover	1764	Bequest of Martin Rusea
Spanish Town, later known as Beckford & Smiths, now St. Jago High	St. Catherine	1743	Bequest of Mrs. Bathshua Beckford
St. James Free	St. James	Before 1826	
St. Catherine Free	St. Catherine	Before 1826	
Titchfield Free	Portland	1785 (boys) 1786 (girls)	Titchfield Trust
Vere Free	Clarendon	Before 1826	
Walton Free later known as Jamaica High School, now Jamaica College in Kingston	St. Ann	1807	Bequest of Charles Drax
Wolmer's Free School	St. Andrew	1729 (boys) 1792 (girls)	Bequest of John Wolmer. 1736 (year of establishment of John Wolmer Trust)

Post-emancipation

Education was viewed as a means of social and economic mobility. Initially, parents sought to have their children gain primary education. Later, they aimed at secondary and tertiary education as these became available. Many young people were apprenticed to tradesmen to learn a trade, in an effort to improve their social mobility and to ensure that they did not have to earn a living from agricultural activity.

Many primary and secondary schools were started by various denominations before government undertook full responsibility. This was especially important in rural areas and to parents who could not afford to pay for their children's education. Many denominations established primary (elementary) schools in close proximity to their churches in the Free Villages. Later they developed secondary schools – some as boarding institutions.

Table 4.2: Some secondary schools established after Emancipation

Name	Parish	Year	Additional Information
Hampton	St. Elizabeth	1855	Funded by Munro & Dickenson Trust by will dated 1797
Happy Grove	Portland	1888	Founded by the Society of Friends (Quakers)
Munro (for boys)	St. Elizabeth	1857	Funded by Munro & Dickenson Trusts by will dated 1797
St. Andrew High School for Girls	St. Andrew	1925	Presbyterian and Methodist churches
St. George's College	Kingston	1850	Roman Catholic Church
St. Hilda's Diocesan High School for Girls	St. Ann	1922	Anglican Church
Westwood High School for Girls	Trelawny	1880	Baptist Church
York Castle (boarding school for boys) now York Castle High School	St. Ann	1876	Methodist Church

1837-1846   The Negro Education Grant was provided by the English Parliament for the education of freed slaves.

1861   Bethlehem Teacher Training College was opened by the Moravians.

1866-1874   Payment of teachers by results was tried.

1868	The Roman Catholic Church started an elementary school for poor boys at Love Lane in Kingston. The school moved to Heywood Street.
1879	The Institute of Jamaica was founded.
1881	The First Jamaica Scholarship was awarded to male student who came first in external examination of the University of Cambridge.
1891	The Great International Exhibition was held at Quebec Hall the present site of Wolmer's Girls' School in Kingston.
1892	A bill was passed in the House of Assembly stating that the government had responsibility for elementary education. An education tax was proposed as part of the bill.
1893	Elementary education was made free for all.
1894	The West India Reference Library was established.
	The Jamaica Union of Teachers (JUT) was formed. Only primary school teachers were members of the union.
1897	St. Joseph's Teacher Training College was established.
1912	The Ward Theatre in Kingston was opened. The theatre was a gift of Charles Ward, Custos of Kingston. It was the fourth theatre built on the site.
1919	West Indies College started by the Seventh-Day Adventist Church in Manchester.
1930s to 1940s	Jamaican sportsmen and sportswomen began to compete in international games.
1941	The Little Theatre Movement (LTM) was formed in Kingston.
1947	The University College of the West Indies (UCWI) was incorporated as a college of the University of London.
1948	The Jamaica Library Service (JLS) was established.
	UCWI opened.

Using Jamaican History in Family Research

1949	*January 4:* The training of nurses commenced at the West Indies School of Nursing on the Mona Campus of UCWI.
1952	The Schools' Library Service was started.
1955	The first National Festival of Arts was held.
1957	Educational reform gave wider access to secondary education. First Common Entrance places were awarded to 10-12 year old children.

Awards were based on the Common Entrance Examination and on the availability of places in existing secondary schools. This replaced the system of government parish scholarships and scholarships granted by private schools.

1958	The University Hospital of the West Indies was opened at Mona.

The Jamaica Institute of Technology was opened – by order of Colonial Government. The name was later changed to College of Arts, Science and Technology (CAST).

1962	The establishment of Public (Government) Secondary schools began.
1965	The Festival Commission for Cultural Development was set up. The work of the Commission broadened in the 1970s and was renamed the Jamaica Cultural Development Commission.
1969	The Student Loan Fund for tertiary education came into operation.
1973	Government announced free secondary and tertiary education as from September, 1974.
1978	The Institute of Jamaica Act provided for the establishment of the National Library.
1979	*April 1:* The National Library commenced operation. It incorporated the West India Reference Library and the Institute of Jamaica.

July 10: The first Reggae Sunsplash was held in Montego Bay.

	The first Caribbean Examination Council examinations were held.
1982	Human Employment and Resource Training (HEART) started.
1987	*February 27:* The School of Art was renamed the Edna Manley School of Visual and Performing Arts. It is the only such school in the Caribbean.
1993	Free secondary education was replaced by cost-sharing.
1999	CAST became the University of Technology (UTECH).
	West Indies College was upgraded to Northern Caribbean University (NCU).

4.4 Freedom and Civil Rights

Perhaps your family has information about members who were involved in the ongoing struggle for civil rights here in Jamaica, in other Caribbean territories and other parts of the world. The family historian would, of course, want to include this information in the family history.

Pre-emancipation

The Jews who came to Jamaica from Europe were looking forward to the freedom of religion that was denied them in Europe. Those who stayed when the English captured the island stayed for the same reason, in spite of the fact that they were denied other civil rights.

Even the English settlers had to be assured of their rights. In 1662 a Royal Proclamation stated that all the children born of English parents in Jamaica were to be regarded as English citizens. Voting rights were limited to white, Protestant males who were 21 years old and over, and who owned or rented property of a specified value. Members of the Assembly had to be much more wealthy. Wives in the colony enjoyed the same rights as those in England.

Inherent in the slave system was the desire and struggle to gain freedom – social, political and economic. Jamaica had its share of freedom fighters – Jews, African slaves, English missionaries, a few planters on the island, and abolitionists in England.

Using Jamaican History in Family Research

1734	Nanny Town, a Maroon settlement, was destroyed by the English.
1739	A peace treaty was signed between the Maroons of the Cockpit Country in the west (led by Cudjoe) and the English (led by Guthrie). The Maroons got land (1500 acres / 607 hectares) free of taxes. Their settlement was named Trelawny Town after the name of the governor. They were also granted the status of 'free people'. In return, the Maroons had to inform the government's superintendent of runaway slaves, capture and hand over such slaves for a reward. The superintendent was to live at Trelawny Town and act as Liaison Officer between the Maroons and the English.
1740	King George of Great Britain granted 'Nanny and her people' and their heirs 100 acres of land in the parish of Portland.
1746	Another slave rebellion took place. Laws were enacted to provide terrible punishments for rebels.
1760	A slave rebellion led by Tacky started in St. Mary and spread to Westmoreland and St. James. 300 slaves and 60 whites were killed. 50 male slaves were hanged. 600 were sent to Belize to be logwood cutters there.
1772	A law passed in England stated that any slave landing in that country was automatically free.
1781	A law was passed in England forbidding the mutilation of slaves (cutting off of ears, hands). The Jamaican slave owners were angry about this 'interference'.
1789	William Wilberforce moved 12 resolutions in the House of Commons (London) against the slave trade.
1795-96	A Second Maroon War was ended by the Pond River Treaty. The cause of the war was a protest by the Maroons against the flogging of two of their number. The governor declared Martial Law and called out the Militia instead of allowing the Superintendent to deal with the matter. A British major offered new land to any Maroons who surrendered. Instead, all those who went from

	Trelawny Town to Montego Bay to surrender were shipped to Nova Scotia, Canada. Three years later they wee taken to Sierra Leone in West Africa.
1807	A law was passed in England to abolish the slave trade.
1816	A law that required planters to pay a fine for every slave they freed was rescinded.
1823	English government instructed Jamaican slave owners to make the conditions of slavery easier. The local House of Assembly objected to this.
1831	The Jews gained full political rights.
1832	The Christmas Rebellion (also called the Baptist War) took place (the last major rebellion before Emancipation) in St. James, Trelawny, Hanover, Westmoreland, St. Elizabeth and Manchester. Sam Sharpe, leader of the Trelawny slaves, claimed 'freedom as a right' thus making the issue one of morality. 200 people were killed and approximately 500 executed. Sam Sharpe was tried and hanged at Montego Bay.
1833	*August 28:* The Abolition Act was passed in London to officially end slavery after a period of apprenticeship.
1834	Adults began a 6-year term of apprenticeship. Children 6 years old and under were freed.
1838	*August 1:* Proclamation from English parliament read at Spanish Town brought slavery to an end. Apprenticeship ended two years early. All apprentices became 'full free'.

Post-emancipation

First Free Village in the British West Indies, Sligoville, started in St. Catherine. Two hundred families who purchased their individual lots settled in the area. Purchase of the land for a village was arranged by Rev. James Philippo, a Baptist minister, in 1835.

Table 4.3 shows the earliest Free Villages.

Table 4.3: Earliest Free Villages

Year	Name and location	Clergyman	Denomination
1838	Philadelphia, St. Ann	Rev. John Clark	Baptist
1838	Sandy Bay, Hanover	Rev. Thomas Burchell	Baptist
1839	Mount Horeb, Hanover	Rev. Hope M. Waddell	Presbyterian
1840	Vale Lionel, Manchester (name changed to Porus)	Rev. James Philippo	Baptist

1865 Social and economic conditions were very bad. Paul Bogle and George William Gordon led the demand of small farmers of St. Thomas for social justice and equality for all before the law. This led to the Morant Bay rebellion.

October: Paul Bogle was caught, tried and hanged for his part in the riots. George William Gordon was also hanged.

1865 Crown Colony government was introduced after the riots. Governor Eyre was dismissed for his poor handling of the situation.

1870-91 This was a period of widespread increase in land purchase by small farmers.

1887 Marcus Garvey was born.

1895 The Jamaica Agricultural Society (JAS) was formed. The society was formed to deal with concerns of small farmers and to improve farming methods by education.

1914 Marcus Garvey founded the Universal Negro Improvement Association (UNIA) in Kingston with the aim of uniting all the negro people of the world and of establishing a country and government of their own.

1918 Some female property owners gained the right to vote.

1919 First act allowing the formation of trade unions was passed.

1929 The People's Political Party was founded by Marcus Garvey. It was the first of its kind.

1934	A.G.S. Coombs formed the Jamaica Workers and Tradesmen Union (JWTU). The union protested low wages and poverty.
1935	Wage workers on the wharves of Kingston and Falmouth agitated for higher pay and better working conditions.
1936	The Jamaica Progressive League first advocated self-government for the island.
1938	People's National Party was launched.
1939	The Bustamante Industrial Trade Union (BITU) founded by Alexander Bustamante was registered as a trade union.
1940	Marcus Garvey died in London.
1943	*July 8:* The Jamaica Labour Party was launched by Alexander Bustamante.
	Universal adult suffrage was declared for all citizens 21 years old and older.
1944	First election under universal adult suffrage for members to the House of Representatives.
1952	The National Workers Union was founded as an affiliate to the People's National Party
1964	Marcus Garvey (1887-1940) was named as the first National Hero.
1965	Paul Bogle (c. 1825-1865) and George William Gordon (1822-1865) were named National Heroes.
1969	Norman Manley (1893-1969) and Alexander Bustamante (1884-1977) were named as National Heroes.
1975	Sam Sharpe and Nanny were named as National Heroes.
1978	The franchise was extended to citizens who were 18 years old.
1997	The Legal Aid Act provided legal aid in criminal and civil cases for those unable to pay their own costs.

4.5 Government

From 1492 to 1962, a period of 470 years, the government of Jamaica was colonial rule. Initially, laws for the colony were made in Spain and England. Under English colonial rule, there was a gradual shift to self-government.

Spanish period 1494-1655

Christopher Columbus reached Jamaica on May 2, 1494. By agreement with the king and queen of Spain, the island was made the private property of Christopher Columbus and his descendants. They took the title Marquis of Jamaica, then a Marquisate of the Spanish empire. This allocation became the basis of a continuing dispute between the Marquises and the Spanish king. The king protected his claim by appointing the governors and lieutenant governors. The governor lived at Villa de la Vega (present Spanish Town), the administrative and judicial capital of the island. The governor appointed all administrative officers and was responsible for the defence of the island. He was assisted by a cabildo (council) of land owners.

British colonial period 1655-1962

The Monarch's representative was a governor. Table 4.4 shows the different forms of government in Jamaica during this period.

Table 4.4: Different forms of government under English rule, 1655-1962

Year	Forms of government	Additional Information
1655-61	Military rule	Period of conflict with Spain
1661	Civil government. An elected Assembly met for the first time in 1663 at Spanish Town	End of military conflict. Assembly could pass laws, but they were subject to approval by the Crown. Voting rights were restricted to male land owners.
1664	Local government	By this time local government in the form of Vestries was established in each parish. Each parish also had a Justice of the Peace (magistrate)

Year	Forms of government	Additional Information
1677-1865	Representative government	Laws passed in England for the colony could be debated but not changed. Only large landowners had the right to vote and be members of the Assembly. Roman Catholics, coloureds, women and slaves were excluded from political life. Jews were excluded until 1831.
1866	Crown Colony Government	The local Assembly lost its right to make laws. The island was under the direct rule of the governor and all laws were made in England. The Vestries were replaced by Municipal Boards. Members were appointed by the governor.
1884	Some steps taken to reestablish representative government	The Assembly was partly elected (on restricted franchise) and partly nominated by the governor.
1885		Municipal and other Boards replaced by a single body – a Parochial Board
1886		Parochial Boards again fully elected (on restricted franchise)
1944		Universal adult suffrage for all citizens over 21 years old for national elections
1947		Adult suffrage extended to local government elections
1956		Name "Parochial Board" changed to "Parish Council"
1957-58	Internal self-government	Island government responsible for all internal affairs; defence and international relations remained with the Crown
1958-61	West Indies Federation	Federation was political union of 10 territories of which Jamaica was one.
1962	Independence	Federation dissolved May 31. Independence on August 6, 1962.

4.6 Land Ownership and Inheritance

The ownership of land was and still is important. In the Pre-emancipation period land ownership, along with ownership of slaves was a sign of desirable social status – that of a free person. During this period and for some time after, land ownership also conferred the right to vote and take part in the political life of the country.

Land ownership was restricted to the Crown (Government), to whites and a few coloureds. Spanish and English governments gave land grants to their nationals to encourage settlement. For example: On December 16, 1661 the king of England issued a proclamation offering 30 acres of land to every male and female over 12 years of age who came to live in the island during the next 2 years. Land grants to military officers were much larger. Small parcels of land were also offered to indentured workers at the end of their indenture.

Two important laws of the period regarding land ownership and inheritance were as follows:

1751   An Act to 'Prevent the Inconvenience Arising from Exorbitant Grants made by White Persons to Negroes'... and to limit such grants was passed. It stated:

Whereas divers large estates consisting of land, cattle stock, money and securities for money, have from time to time been left by white persons to mulattos, and other offspring of mulattos, not being their own issue born in lawful wedlock

And whereas such bequests tend greatly to destroy the distinction requisite, and absolutely necessary, to be kept up in this island between white persons and Negroes their issue and their offspring, and may in progress of time be the means of decreasing the number of white inhabitants in the island

And whereas it is the policy of every good government to restrain individuals from disposing of their property, to the particular prejudice and detriment of their heirs and relations, and of the injury and of the community in general

Be it therefore enacted... that... from and after the first

> day of January, which will be in the year of Our Lord, 1752, no lands, negro, mulatto or other slave, cattle stock, money or other real estate in this island whatsoever, shall be given, granted to, or declared to be in trust for, or to the use of, or devised by any white person to any whatever, or to any mulatto, or other persons not being their own issue born in lawful wedlock, and being the issue of a negro.

1762   The Jamaica Inheritance Act placed a limit of two thousand pounds on the value of property that a free coloured person could inherit from a white. Any will that exceeded that amount was null and void.

Post-emancipation

After Emancipation, free people began to become landowners. The Baptist, Moravian and Presbyterian Churches are on record for purchasing large estates, subdividing and selling small holdings to the newly freed. The Crossman Commission (1882) and the Norman Commission (1897) endorsed the establishment of small holdings. Some of the land that was available to small holders were marginal hillside lands. Land settlement schemes and the creation of residential subdivisions have allowed more persons to own land. The establishment of the National Housing Trust has increased the range of income groups with access to funds to purchase homes and lots for building homes.

1888   Registration of Titles Law passed. Registration began October 1, 1889.

4.7 Migration Patterns

Jamaica's population, like that of all the other countries in the new world is largely made up of peoples from the old world. Immigrants came and still come; emigrants continue to leave.

Pre-emancipation immigration

The earliest known immigrants were the Taino Indians – a nation tribe of the Americas. There are about 150 sites in Jamaica where they are known to have lived.

The years 1494-1834 were the times when the largest number of other immigrants came to the island from the old world continents of Europe and Africa. Once apprenticeship began, planters began to seek replacements for African labour. Europeans were preferred since the local European were greatly outnumbered in relation to the Africans. Between 1834 and 1845 about 41,000 came to the island from Germany, Scotland, England, Portugal and Ireland. Some found agricultural work not to their liking, so they left the plantations for the towns or went off to the United States of America.

1492/1502 Start of Spanish immigration.

1513 The first Africans were brought in by a French company given permission by the King of Spain.

1580-1640 The first Jews came from Spain and Portugal some via England, France, Holland and Germany.

1655 Start of British immigration from Britain and other British colonies.

1656 1500 British settlers came from Nevis to the area near Port Morant, St. Thomas.

1662 1000 British settlers came from Barbados with the new governor, Lord Modyford.

More Jews came from Brazil and from England.

1664 Some Jews came from Cayenne (French Guiana).

1667 1200 Jews came from Surinam after the Dutch seized the territory.

1672 English-owned Royal Africa Company entered the slave trade to the Caribbean including Jamaica.

1698-1700 Scottish immigrants came from a failed Scottish colony, Darien, Panama, to St. Elizabeth and parts of now Westmoreland. Some sold themselves as servants to plantations.

1700-1800 More Jews came from the Dutch island of Curaçao and from Germany.

1716-17 Immigrants came from Scotland.

1747 More Scots were exiled to the island following the defeat at Culloden by the English when some tried to restore a Stuart (Scottish) king to the English throne. They settled in St. Thomas-in-the-East, St. Elizabeth, St. James, Westmoreland, Clarendon, St. Ann, St. Catherine, Hanover, St. Mary. By mid-century one third of all white colonists were Scottish.

1775 American loyalists opposed to American independence from Britain came with their slaves mainly to St. Elizabeth.

1791-1803 French Royalists came from Haiti with their slaves. These Royalists were opposed to the independence of Haiti from France and fled the slave revolution for independence.

1807 Official end of slave trade.

1833-1836 Irish immigrants came from Ballymoney (1833) to St. Ann, and from Belfast, County Antrim (1835) to Brown's Town, St. Ann.

Table 4.5 gives information about German immigration between 1834 and 1837.

Table 4.5: Some pre-emancipation German immigration

Date	No. of immigrants	From	To
May 1834	64	Bremen	Portland: Pleasant Mount
Dec. 1834	65	Bremen	*St. Ann* – St. Ann's Bay, Dry Harbour Mountain *St. Elizabeth* – Black River, Lacovia *St. James* – Montego Bay *Trelawny* – Rio Bueno
Dec. 1835 and 1837	532 250	Westphalia and Waldeck	*St. Ann* – Middlesex (near Guy's Hill) *Portland* – Altamont (near Hope Bay) *St. James* – Montego Bay to estates in the west *Trelawny* – areas around Rio Bueno *Westmoreland* – Seaford Town

The continuous stream of European and African peoples resulted in an increased population. Table 4.6 shows the distribution of the main population groups.

Table 4.6: Distribution of population by ethnic groups, 1690-1830

Year	European	African	Coloured
1690	7,000	34,000	n/a
1710	7,000	49,000	1,000
1750	8,000	80,000	4,000
1760	11,000	122,000	9,000
1770	17,000	185,000	23,000
1790	25,000	250,000	32,000
1810	30,000	325,000	55,000
1830	30,000	312,000	60,000

Post-emancipation immigration

After Emancipation small numbers of immigrants came mainly to replace African labourers who left the plantations. These immigrants were people from Sierra Leone, Europe, China, India. Between 1837 and 1841 these also included Scots (to St. Elizabeth, Portland and St. Ann), Germans, Portuguese and Irish (to St. Ann).

In 1841, the S.S. William Pirrie sailed from Stranraer, Scotland with Irish and Scottish migrants to settle in Jamaica. They came as agents, attorneys, merchants and shopkeepers.

1844   Act XXI permitted Indian immigration into Jamaica

Tables 4.7 to 4.9 detail the immigrants from Africa, China and India.

The number of Jews in the island increased toward the end of the nineteenth century and at the beginning of the twentieth century with arrivals from Egypt, Syria, Czechoslovakia, Austria, Poland and Russia.

The Jews, the Lebanese and some Indians formed a group of immigrants independent of the plantations.

Table 4.7: Indentured workers from Africa, 1840-1865

Number of Immigrants	From	To
10,000	Congo, Kroo Coast, St. Helena, Sierra Leone	Clarendon, Hanover (Cascade), Metcalfe, St. James, St. Mary, St. Thomas (Amity Hall & Rhine estates), Vere, Westmoreland

Table 4.8: Dates of arrival of Chinese indentured workers, 1854-1888

Year	Country of Origin	Number	Additional Information
1854	Hong Kong	267	Ship: 'Epsom'
1854	Panama	205	Ships: 'Vampire' and 'Theresa Jane'
1860s	Trinidad & Guyana	200	Came as indentured workers on 3 year contract
1884	China	680	
After 1885	China	700	
1888	China	800	

Table 4.9: Indentured workers from India, 1845-1914

Year	Region of Origin
1845	Chota Nagpur division of Bengal Providency
1860s-1870s	Most came from the Northern Provinces, Bihar Oudh. Smaller numbers came from Agra, Central India and Nepal
1880s	
1891	Two thirds came from Northwest Provinces and Oudh and others from Bengal and Bihar
After 1902	Northwest Provinces United Provinces of Agra and Oudh

Using Jamaican History in Family Research

Pre-emancipation emigration

From 1655 onwards there was a small but continuous stream of emigrants out of the island. Some Spaniards fled to Cuba when the island was taken by the British. Some British small farmers went off to Honduras in Central America to make their living by logwood cutting.

Post-emancipation emigration

After Emancipation there was heavier emigration than before. People began to leave the island in search of economic and social opportunities. Some were British who left their failed plantations, others were newly freed persons who migrated mainly to countries in the Caribbean region like Cuba, Panama and Costa Rica. Some went to the United States of America.

In 1849 some left to seek their fortunes in the gold rush in California. In 1852, others went off to Australia for the same purpose – to search for gold in New South Wales. Some followed the trade routes to the east coasts of the United States of America and Canada.

The Gleaner of July 7, 2000 stated that Jamaican emigrants were scattered abroad as far as Lebanon, Germany, Japan, Norway, Sweden, Denmark, and some countries of the African continent.

1850-55   Jamaicans went to Panama to work on the railroad.

1871-90   Some Jamaicans went to Costa Rica to build the railroad from San José, on the Caribbean Sea to the capital, Porto Limón. Others went to work on banana plantations both in Costa Rica and Nicaragua.

1881-89   85,000 Jamaicans worked for Ferdinand DeLesseps in his unsuccessful attempt to build a Panama Canal.

1889   *March 22:* Jamaicans returned from Panama because work on the canal ceased.

1902   Work on Panama Canal restarted by United States of America. Many Jamaicans went to work.

1914   World War I started.

1915   *November:* A total of 500 men volunteered to go to Britain to join the armed forces.

1918	World War I ended. Some Jamaicans remained in Britain; some returned to the island.
1920	Many Jamaicans migrated to Cuba in search of jobs on plantations, on the railroad and in domestic service.
1929	The last Indian repatriates left the island.
1939	Outbreak of World War II. Jamaicans went to Britain to join the armed forces or to work in factories to support the war.
1940	*April 28:* 40 Jamaican carpenters left to work in the Canal Zone, Panama.
1943	*April 5:* An agreement for the Farm Workers Programme to the United States of America was signed between the Government of Jamaica and the United States Department and the Department of Agriculture.
1944	An agreement was made under which female domestic workers went to the United States of America. World War II ended.
1950s-60s	Large emigration to Britain after the war as follows:

1956	17,000 plus	1959	123,796
1957	13,087	1960	32,060
1958	9,992	1961	39,000 plus

1966	Canadian Seasonal Workers Programme commenced.
1970s onwards	Continuous migration to the United States of America especially to Tampa and Miami in Florida State and to Canada – mainly Toronto – and to Britain

4.8 Money

The currency of the island changed over time. Many documents required stamps (e.g receipts) and others showed prices of goods and property. The following information will help the family historian to place these documents in time.

The Spanish used a silver dollar which was the international currency much as the American dollar is today. Eight reals (pronounced ree-als) made 1 dollar; 11 cuartos made 1 real. The English continued using the Spanish dollar up until the early nineteenth century, when they gradually introduced the Sterling system. Over time, a Jamaican currency emerged.

1825   Two British silver coins were introduced – threepence and penny-half-penny. (The penny-half-penny was half of a threepence.) Half threepence was called a 'Christian quattie' (from cuarto?) since it was commonly used for collection in the church.

1837   The first bank notes were issued by different banks.

1844   Moneys in circulation in addition to sterling (British money – pounds, guineas, shillings, pennies / pence) were gold dubloons and silver dollars of Spain, Mexico and Colombia. All were legal tender in the island. A doubloon was worth 64 shillings and the dollar was worth four shillings and twopence.

1869   *July:* Two Jamaican coins (sterling) were minted – pennies and half-pennies. They bore the Jamaican crest on one side and the monarch on the other.

1880   Farthing coins were minted. A farthing was one quarter of a penny.

1889   The Bank of Nova Scotia (BNS) of Canada opened its first branch in Jamaica, in Kingston.

1920   The Canadian Bank of Commerce (CBC) opened its first branch.

The Government of Jamaica issued its first bank notes – ten shillings, five shillings and two shillings and sixpence (two shillings and six-pence was half of five shillings). Prior to this individual banks issued their own bank notes.

1942   The Government of Jamaica issued more of its own bank notes – one pound and five pound.

1960   The Bank of Jamaica was given the sole right and responsibility for issuing Jamaican currency. The bank issued five shilling, ten shilling, one pound and five pound notes with the signature of the Governor of the Bank of Jamaica on all notes.

1969 Jamaica's currency changed from sterling to dollars and cents. Coins were minted with Jamaica's Coat-of-arms on one side and a national hero on the other. The first decimal coin – a five cent – was minted with the Jamaica crocodile on one side and the Jamaica Coat-of-Arms on the other.

1970 Sterling ceased to be legal tender in the country.

1971 The Jamaica National Building Society started as a merger of 4 Building Societies. Operation began with 8 offices in 7 parishes.

1994 Five hundred dollar note introduced by Bank of Jamaica

2000 Thousand dollar note introduced by Bank of Jamaica

4.9 Natural Hazards

From time to time, Jamaica suffered from earthquakes, droughts, hurricanes and epidemics. These natural hazards impacted families in different ways – deaths, loss of property, loss of documents, internal and external migration. Perhaps members of your family were involved and/or heard about them. Newspapers and other written material carried details about people and places and are therefore valuable resource material. Some of the most devastating are listed below.

1692 Port Royal was almost completely destroyed by an earthquake. A large part of the city sank. Many people moved to Kingston to live. This was the beginning of its becoming the capital.

1703 What was left of Port Royal was destroyed by fire.

1850 Outbreak of Asiatic cholera in which 32,000 persons died.

1855-65 Island affected by an outbreak of small pox and by droughts and floods. These disasters added to the general distress that led up to the Morant Bay riots.

1887-88 There was an outbreak of small pox.

1907 The capital of the island, Kingston, was partially destroyed by earthquake and a subsequent fire.

1918   There was an outbreak of Spanish influenza in which hundreds died.

1951   Hurricane Charlie – the worst hurricane in 70 years – swept over the island. One hundred and fifty persons lost their lives and there was enormous damage to property.

1988   Hurricane Gilbert – one of the most powerful hurricanes ever recorded – swept over the entire island causing much damage and the loss of some forty-five lives.

2004   Hurricane Ivan, a category 4-5 hurricane, passed south of Jamaica, lashed the island for almost 24 hours. Fourteen persons died. Hardest hit were the southern parishes. Storm surges of 4-5 metres in some places (e.g., Portland Cottage, Clarendon) did much damage to coastal areas).

4.10 Religion

Religion has been important in Jamaica's history. Christianity has been and still is the dominant religion. It has been said that Jamaica has more churches per square kilometer than any other country in the world.

The Roman Catholic denomination came with the Spaniards in 1494. A charitable lay (non-clerical) organization, the Confradia, provided hospitals and orphanages. The Roman Catholic remained the state church until 1655 when the British invaded the island. The denomination was revived in 1792 when clergy came from France, Haiti, Colombia and England to serve the Roman Catholic congregations living here.

Jewish immigrants brought Judaism because they enjoyed freedom of religion here – a privilege that was denied them in Spain and Portugal at the time.

Under British rule the Church of England (the Anglican Church) became the state church and remained so until 1870. The non-Anglican denominations (the Dissenters) came in the 1800s. While some missionaries sought to have slaves conform to slavery, others viewed slavery as unjust and inhumane. The government of the day placed restrictions on the activities of the latter since they were opposed to the existing system of slavery.

Pre-emancipation

1494 Spanish established Roman Catholicism as the state church.

1511 King Ferdinand of Spain called for Catholic education of slaves.

1580-1640 This was a period of great migration of Jews from Spain and Portugal. Some came to Jamaica and brought Judaism.

1748 Church of England (Anglican Church) was established as the state religion under the Bishop of London.

1754 The Moravian mission started work in the island in St. Elizabeth.

1782 Leile and Baker, two slaves who came from the United States of America with their loyalist masters started the Native Baptist Church.

1789 Rev. Thomas Coke a visiting Methodist Minister from England preached in Kingston. He recommended the formation of a Methodist society in the island.

1790 Rev. Hammett formed the first Jamaican Methodist Society in Hannah Town.

1792 Roman Catholic Church re-established by French and Spanish refugees.

1807 The Common Council of Kingston passed an order forbidding all except authorized ministers of religion (Anglican) from 'preaching, teaching, praying, singing psalms in any meeting of negroes or coloured people'. The order also detailed the punishments for whites and slaves who broke the law.

1814 The English Baptist mission started work in the island.

1824 The Presbyterian mission began.

An Anglican see, the bishopric of Jamaica, was created.

1835 Other missionary groups operating were:

- Society for the Propagation of the Gospel
- The London Missionary Society
- The Church Missionary Society

Post-emancipation

Since Emancipation many other denominations and religions came to Jamaica. Many denominations were branches of churches in the United States of America and England. Some local denominations also started. Foremost among them was the Rastafarian religion.

Indian indentured workers brought the Hindu religion. Islam was brought by some African slaves, but the stronger introduction was made by the Indians. Between 1911 and 1912 the following distribution among Indians was found to be: 52.99% Hindus; 3.86% were Muslim; 0.59% were Buddhist; 29% were Christian.

(*Source:* Shepherd p.16. Extract from 'Abstract O', Protector of Immigration Papers, 1911-12 p.78).

1843   The Baptists opened Calabar Theological College, at Rio Bueno, Trelawny, to train ministers for service in Jamaica and Africa.

1845   Presbyterians opened an academy in Montego Bay to train ministers for Jamaica and for Calabar, West Africa.

1869   Calabar Theological College was moved to Kingston.

1870   The Church of England was disestablished, that is, it was no longer the state church supported by government.

1882   Salvation Army started work.

1932   Foundation was laid for the Salvation Central Hall in memory of its founder (General Boothe) at Parade, Kingston.

1970   A Hindu temple was built on Hagley Park Road

References for further reading

This list provides readers with material to complement the Historical notes.

Beckles, Hilary McD., *Centering Women: Gender Discourses in the Caribbean Slave Society*. Ian Randle Publishers, Kingston, Jamaica, 2000

Binney, Marcus, Harris, John, Martin, Kit, (ed.) Marguerite Curtin, *Jamaica's Heritage – An Untapped Resource*. Mill Press, Kingston, Jamaica 1991.

Black, Clinton V., *History of Jamaica*, Collins Educational, 1983.

Braithwaite E., *The Development of Creole Society in Jamaica 1770-1820*. Oxford: Clarendon Press, 1971.

Bryan, Patrick, *The Jamaican People 1880-1902*. First published by MacMillan, 1991 and then by University of the West Indies Press, 2000.

Buisseret, David, with photographs by J. Tyndale Biscoe and cartography by Tom Willcockson, *Historic Jamaica from the Air*. Caribbean University Press, 1969.

Bush, Barbara, *Slave Women in Caribbean Society 1650-1838*. James Curry, London, 1990.

Cundall, Frank, *Jamaican Place Names*. Institute of Jamaica 1909

Cundall, Frank, *Catalogue of Portraits in Jamaica's Historic Gallery*. Institute of Jamaica, Kingston, Jamaica, 1914.

Ingram, Kenneth E.N., *Manuscript Sources for the History of the West Indies with special reference to Jamaica in the National Library of Jamaica and Supplementary Sources in the West Indies, North America, the United Kingdom and Elsewhere*. University of the West Indies Press, 2000.

Ingram, Kenneth E.N., *Sources of Jamaican History 1655-1838: A Bibliographical Survey with particular reference to Manuscript Sources*. Zug, Switzerland, 1976.

Lampe, Armando (ed), *Christianity in the Caribbean: Essays in Church History*. University of the West Indies Press, 2001.

Long, Edward, *The History of Jamaica*. Cass Library of West Indies Studies

Nettleford, Rex, *Caribbean Cultural Identity: The Case of Jamaica*. Institute of Jamaica, Kingston, Jamaica, 1987

Senior, Olive, *A – Z of Jamaican Heritage*. Heinemann Educational Books (Caribbean) Ltd. and The Gleaner Company Ltd., 1983. (See African Heritage, Maroons, Free Africans)

Shepherd, Verene, *Women in Caribbean History*. Ian Randle Publishers Kingston, Jamaica 2000

Sherlock, Philip and Bennett, Hazel, *The Story of the Jamaican People*. Ian Randle Publishers Ltd., in collaboration with Creative Production and Training Centre Ltd. (CPTC) Kingston, Jamaica 1988

Sibley, Inez, *Dictionary of Place Names in Jamaica*. Institute of Jamaica, 1978

Simmonds, Lorna, 'Slave Higglering in Jamaica, 1780-1834'. *Jamaica Journal*, Vol. 20 No. 1, Feb.-April 1987. Institute of Jamaica, Kingston, Jamaica.

Family Data for Future Generations

When you have completed your family tree and/or history and recognized the value of it, you will want to ensure continuity of the work. You may find the following suggestions helpful.

Collecting information

- Encourage the collection of family memorabilia such as letters, diaries, family Bibles, orders of services for family occasions (christenings, baptisms, weddings, anniversaries, funerals) eulogies and tributes from friends and co-workers.
- Encourage the taking of family photographs with the identity of persons written on the back of the photographs or on labels in family albums. Include information on what the photographs shows, when and where it was taken. Explain any significant features of the photographs.
- Include information on the family keepsakes or treasures telling who the owners were and how they were acquired. Share photographs of valuables. Put away these family treasures in a safe place.
- Become a good listener. Listen to the elderly. As they get older, some may lose short-term memory, but are good at recounting, repetitively, information about their early years. The information is usually correct.

Family Data for Future Generations

- At family get-togethers, tape record or videotape the speeches and views of those present about the occasion. Some older family members may offer to share their memories of past events. Share these recordings at another family occasion.

Storing materials

- Original material should be kept in a safe place. The location should be one secure from moisture and the possibility of water damage. A fireproof environment is also essential.
- Photocopy material and store in a different place from originals. This may involve giving photographs of original material to other family members for safe keeping. Some communities have libraries or archives that collect family history material. Find out if such facilities are available in your area. Some libraries will agree not to allow public access to material without the consent of the owner family.

Passing on the job

Get younger family members interested and willing to continue the history. You could set up a small committee so that you may stimulate each other, keep the interest high and establish a tradition.

Purchase a Family History Computer Programme. It allows easy recording, organizing and sharing of data. Always make copies of your family history material. Print hard copies at regular intervals to ensure, that, in the event of computer problems, data is not lost. But, do not be discouraged if you do not have access to a computer. Begin recording and sharing information using the suggestions in this book. That is how I started some twenty years ago.

APPENDIX

Maps

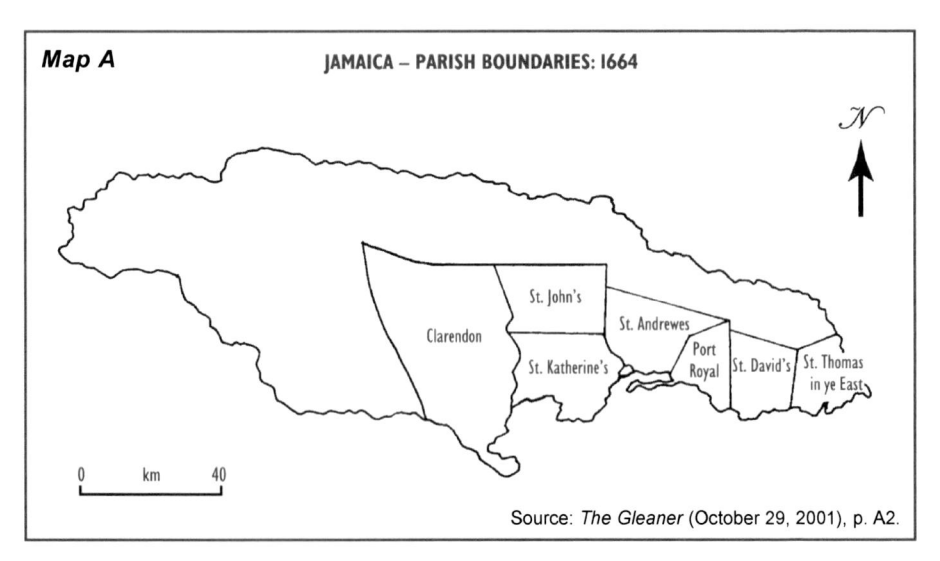

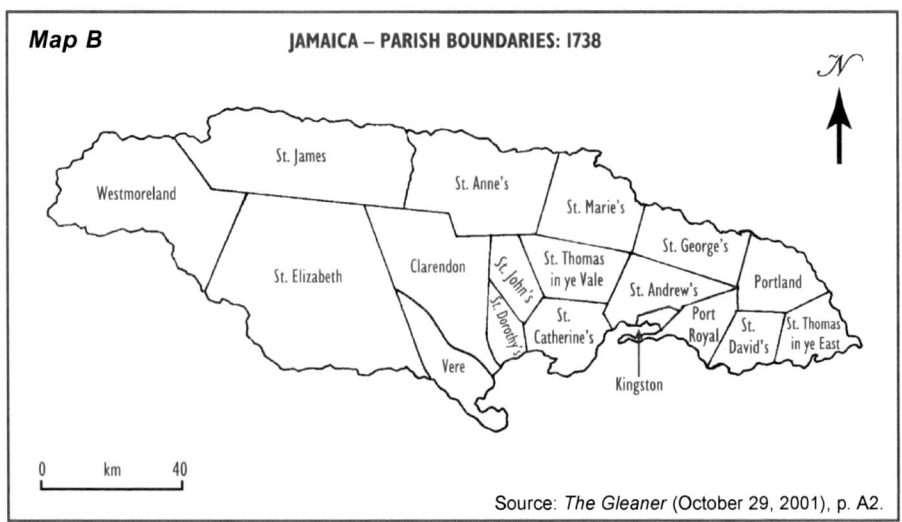

Map A — JAMAICA – PARISH BOUNDARIES: 1664

Parishes shown: Clarendon, St. John's, St. Katherine's, St. Andrewes, Port Royal, St. David's, St. Thomas in ye East.

0 km 40

Source: *The Gleaner* (October 29, 2001), p. A2.

Map B — JAMAICA – PARISH BOUNDARIES: 1738

Parishes shown: Westmoreland, St. James, St. Anne's, St. Marie's, St. George's, St. Elizabeth, Clarendon, St. John's, St. Thomas in ye Vale, St. Andrew's, Portland, St. Dorothy's, Vere, St. Catherine's, Kingston, Port Royal, St. David's, St. Thomas in ye East.

0 km 40

Source: *The Gleaner* (October 29, 2001), p. A2.

Maps

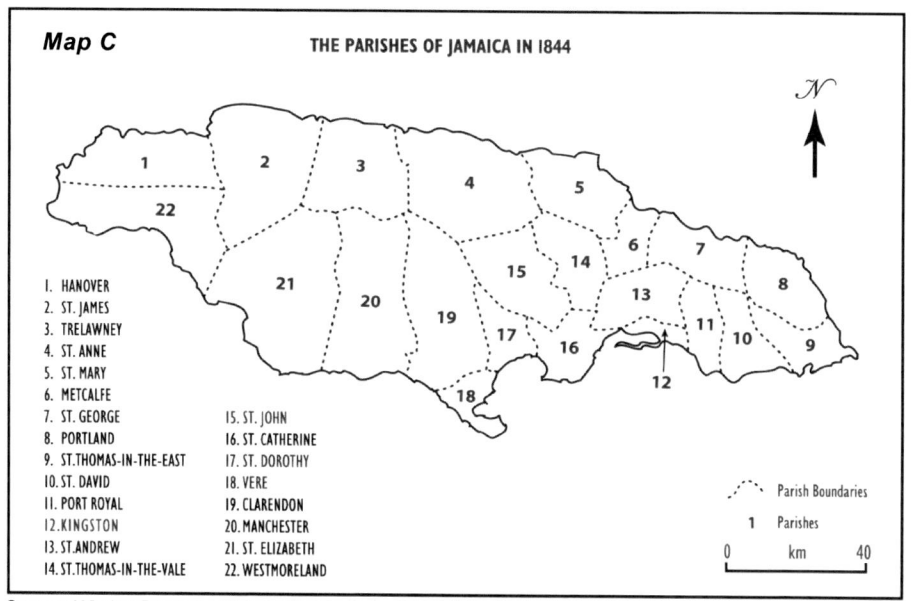

Map C THE PARISHES OF JAMAICA IN 1844

1. HANOVER
2. ST. JAMES
3. TRELAWNEY
4. ST. ANNE
5. ST. MARY
6. METCALFE
7. ST. GEORGE
8. PORTLAND
9. ST. THOMAS-IN-THE-EAST
10. ST. DAVID
11. PORT ROYAL
12. KINGSTON
13. ST. ANDREW
14. ST. THOMAS-IN-THE-VALE
15. ST. JOHN
16. ST. CATHERINE
17. ST. DOROTHY
18. VERE
19. CLARENDON
20. MANCHESTER
21. ST. ELIZABETH
22. WESTMORELAND

Source: Wintlett Browne and Paulette Dunn-Smith, *The Parishes of Jamaica* (Kingston: Carlong Publishers (Caribbean) Limited, 1994), p.8.

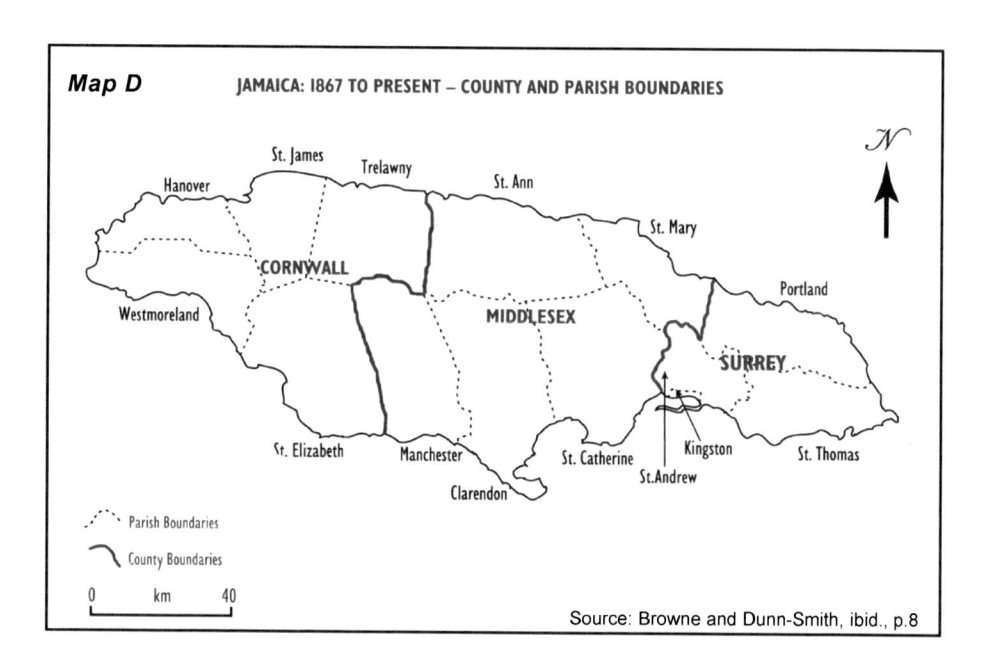

Map D JAMAICA: 1867 TO PRESENT – COUNTY AND PARISH BOUNDARIES

Source: Browne and Dunn-Smith, ibid., p.8

121

Select Bibliography

Andrade, Jacob A.P.M. 1941. *A Record of the Jews in Jamaica from the English Conquest to the Present Times*. The Jamaica Times Ltd., 8-12 King Street, Kingston, Jamaica B.W.I.

Chen Julie. 2004. The Chinese in Jamaica – 150 Years of Nation Building - 1854-2004 in Celebrating Chinese New Year, January 22, 2004. The Year of the Monkey. A *Gleaner* Supplement.

Craton, Michael. 1975. Jamaican Slavery. In *Race and Slavery in the Western Hemisphere*. Princeton. pp.249-84.

Craton, Michael. 1978. *Searching for the Invisible Man*. Harvard University Press.

Fremmer, Ray. 1988. The People of Seaford Town. *The Jamaican* No.2, Vol.11. A Ravrie Publication.

Higman, B.W. 1988. *"Jamaica Surveyed" – Plantation Maps and Plans of Eighteenth and Nineteenth Centuries*. Institute of Jamaica Publications Ltd.

Lyew-Ayee, Parris A. 2004. Call me 'Mr. Chin'. In Celebrating Chinese New Year, January 22, 2004. The Year of the Monkey. A *Gleaner* Supplement.

Mitchell Madeleine B. 1988. *Jamaican Ancestry: How to Find Out More*. Heritage Books, Inc. Maryland, USA.

Mullally, Robert. 1997. 'The Irish in Jamaica (Excerpts of a speech given at the St. Patrick's Day Celebration "Drowning the Shamrock" at the Wyndham Kingston Hotel). *The Jamaica Herald*, magazine supplement 'Pure Class', April 20, 1997.

Poxon, John Coke. 1989. *The Man and His Mission*. Bicentenary Publication.

Select Bibliography

Schuler, Monica. 1980. "Alas, alas, Kongo": A social history of indentured African immigration into Jamaica, 1841-1865. Baltimore: Johns Hopkins Press. Seaford Town advertising feature. *The Gleaner* August 14, 2003.

Senior, Olive. 1983. *A – Z of Jamaican Heritage*. Heinemann Educational Books (Caribbean) Ltd. and The Gleaner Company Ltd.

Shepherd, Verene. 1994. *Transients to Settlers – The Experiences of Indians in Jamaica 1845-1950*. Centre of Research in Asian Immigration, the University of Warwick and Peepal Tree Books.

Sherlock, Philip and Hazel Bennett. 1988. *The Story of the Jamaican People*. Ian Randle Publishers Ltd. In collaboration with Creative Production and Training Centre Ltd. (CPTC) Kingston, Jamaica.

Sibley, Inez. 1978. *Dictionary of Place Names in Jamaica*. Institute of Jamaica.

The Jamaica Defence Force. 2002. Historical Overview of the Jamaica Defence Force, September 2002. http://www.jdfmil.org/index.html

Thomas, Mary Elizabeth. 1974. *Jamaica and Voluntary Laborers from Africa 1840-1865*. Gainsville University Press of Florida.

Tortello Rebecca. 2003. The arrival of the Irish in Jamaica. Out of many one cultures. The people who came. *The Gleaner*, December 1, 2003.

Tortello, Rebecca. 2002. The Arrival of the Chinese. *The Jamaica Gleaner:* Pieces of the Past 06/03/02.

Index of Sources, Documents, Genealogy Sources, Laws

Abolition Act 98
adoption(s) 45
 - certificates 39
African(s) 53, 55, 59, 63, 75-76, 78-80, 96, 105, 107
 - heritage 44
 - labour 105, 107
 - women 76, 79
 - Free 63-65
African-Caribbean Institute of Jamaica / Jamaica Memory Bank 49
African place names 75
 - Calabar 115
Air Jamaica Ltd. 88
airmail postal service 87
American 89
 - loyalist 106
 - Revolutionary War 32
 - War of Independence 65
Alexandria, St. Ann 64
Amity Hall 65
Amity Hall Estate 108
ancestor(s) 4,14,17,24,31, 33,35,36,37,49,51,53, 55,60,70,71,75,84,85
ancestry 5,55,57,65,71, 77,79,84
Angels, St. Catherine 86
Anglican / Church of England 24,25,27,28,30, 32,38,77,78,80,93,113, 114
Anglican Diocese of Jamaica 25
apprentices 78,98
Argyle, Hanover 65
army 88
 - barracks 32
 - officers 55

Australia 109
awards 14,18,19,33-34,35,95
Bahamas, The 98
banana trade 87
bank - bank notes 111
baptismal (Christening) 66,78
 - certificates 9
Baptist 24,26,61-63,98,99,115
 - church 65,93,104,114
 - native 25
 - English 25
Barbados 56,73,106
bastard(s) 79,80,81
Bastardy Act/Affiliation Law 81
Beckford and Smith (now St. Jago High) 92
Belize 97
Bethlehem Teacher Training College 93
bills of sale 39
birth 40,42
 - certificates 39,77
 - records 66,72,78
 - registration 76,81
Bogle, Paul 99,100
Britain 53,97,105,106, 109,110
British 55,56,57
 - armed forces 88,90
 - awards 34
 - immigration 105-106
 - military records 32
 - naval officers 32,55
 - ports 36
 - records 32,33,57
 - Royal Artillery 32
 - Royal Navy 32
 - soldiers 32
British West Indies 31

Brown's Town, St. Ann x,56,106
Buff Bay, Portland x
building society 112
burial traditions 82
 - African
 - European 82
 - Hindu 82
 - Jewish
 - Muslim
business directories 41,42
Bustamante Industrial Trade Union (BITU) 100
Cable and Wireless 88
Calabar Theological College 115
California 109
Cambridge examinations 42
Canada 57,64,70,87, 89,98,109,110,111
Canadian seasonal worker programme 110
Caribbean 51,*54*,55,67,96, 106,109
Caribbean Examination Council *see* Examination Council
Cascade, Hanover 108
CAST *see* College of Arts, Science and Technology
Caymanas Estate, St. Catherine 70
cemetery(/ies) 29-30,32
 - Chinese 70,82
 - Jewish 30,57,82
 - public 82
 - records 29
cenotaph memorials 29,30
certificate 14,19,22,38
 - of No Impediment 80
 - birth 9,19,28,39,77

124

Index

- baptismal (christening) 9
- marriage 9,19,28,39
Chapelton, Clarendon *x*
Chester Castle, Hanover 65
child-rearing 79
children
 - born out of wedlock 76
 - Status of Children Act 81
China *54*,69,70,73,81, 107,108
Chinese 53,55,69,70,74, 76,77,81
 - Benevolent Association Ltd. 70
 - cemetery 70,82
 - Cultural Association 70
 - extended family 81
 - Hakka Conference 70
 - history and culture 37
 - households 81
 - indentured workers 69,108
 - independent immigrants 70
 - merchants 69
 - migration 80
 - settlements 70
 - shopkeepers 69
 - sweethearts 81
Chinese Public News 43
cholera 67,112
Christening / baptism 3,12, 19,23,27,29,76,118
Christian
 - denominations 24,25, 55,85
 - ministers 27,78,80,114, 115
 - religion 76,83,85,96, 113-115
Christian / first names 8,76
Christianity 113
Christmas Rebellion / Baptist War 98
Chung San News 43
church(es)
 - buildings 38,39
 - cemeteries 29,40,82
 - magazines 19,23
 - programmes 19,23
Church of England (Anglican) 113,114
 - records 38
 - registers 38,42

Church of God of Jamaica 25
Church of Jesus Christ of the Latter-Day Saints 27
circumcisions 26,27
citations 19
citizenship
 - certificates of 39
 - dual 4
 - naturalized 2
civil registration 18,27, 28,38
civil rights 83,96
Clarendon 25,26,*68*,70, 92,106,108,113,*120*,*121*
Clarendon Park 87
Clarks Town, Trelawney *x*,75
Cockpit country 97
Coley estates 70
Collector General 23
Collector of Taxes 23
collectorate(s) 23
College of Arts, Science and Technology 35,95
see The University of Technology
coloureds 20,31,44,78,113
 - population 44,73,74,79
 - Free Persons 78
Commissioner of Police 100
Common Council of Kingston 114
Common Entrance Examination 84,95
common law unions 79
common-law titles 20,22,23
community 3,4,8,16,19, 28,34,36,41,49,76,103
Congo 108
Congolese 65
congregational churches 24,25
Constant Spring estate 70
Content, Hanover 65
contract / indentured workers 64,67,69, 70,108
conveyances 20,22,23,39
Copse, Hanover 65
cornerstones 29
Cornwall 31,75,*121*
Cornwall Chronicle 43

Cornwall Courier 44
Costa Rica
 - San José 109
court(s) 19,20,22,38, 45-47,52
cremation 29,82
Creole 78
Crossman Commission 104
crown colony government 99,102
crown lands 22,103
Cuba 73,87,109,110
Cudjoe 97
Daily News 29
Damascus 71
death
 - announcements 3,36
 - certificates 9,19,38,39
 - registration 24,27,28,81
deeds 23,39,43,66,77
denomination(s) 24,25,26, 28,29,55,60-62,63,80,8 5,93,99,113,115,
descendants 24,32,55, 64,101
Diocese of Jamaica 25,26
Disciples of Christ 24,25
Discovery Bay *x*
dissenter(s) 28,78,80,113
 - births 26
 - deaths 26
 - denominations 26
 - marriages 26
 - records 26,27,28,
divorce 45,46,80,82
drought 69,84,112
Dry Harbour Mountains 64,105
earthquake 57,84,112
East Indian(s) 67,74
 - estates 67
 - family systems 80
 - immigrants 80,84
 - inherit (property) 80
 - marriage 80
Edna Manley School of Visual and Performing Arts (School of Art) 96
education 99,114
 - elementary 94
 - freed slaves 93
 - secondary 92,95,96
 - tertiary 92,95
education and culture 91-96

125

educational
- documents / reports 19-20
emigration: destinations of Jamaicans 109-110
English 58
- colonists /citizens 22,55
Esquivel, Juan de
estate 103-104
- burial grounds 29,32
- documents 36
- layout 43
- maps 57,60
- overseers 55
- owners 20,29,44,55,76
- records 29,43
- slaves: categories 60
- Indian immigrants 67,67
ethnicity 6,53,74,76,77
Etu 65
eulogy 19,118
European
- settlers 56,88,96,106
Ewarton, St.Catherine x,87
Examination Council 35,96
executors / executrix 20
Falmouth, Trewlawny x,30,44,61,62,75,86,100
Falmouth Gazette 44
Falmouth Post 44
family 2,49,69,75,79, 84,96,119
- bibles 19,76,118
- court 46,81
- extended 2,4,79,81
- friends 2,3,8,19,37
- gathering 3,12
- 'get-together' 12,119
- historian 18,29,35,37, 38,39,41,47,47,52,55, 57,65,74,76,85,96
- land 23,45
- letters 19,51,66,77
- life 1,53,55,78-82
- members 1,2,3,4,5,6,8, 9,12,13,14-15,18,19,20, 29,33,36,39,40,45,51, 70,82,84,85,88,112,119
- newsletter 12,15
- personal papers 18
- photographs 12,19,118
- plots 29,30,82
- property 20
- reunion 3,12-15
- story(ies) 1,9,12

- tree 3,4,5,8,9,*10-11*,12, 14,17,39,51,118
Family History Centre 27
Farm Workers Programme (USA) 110
father(s)
- name 76,77
Federation of Family History Societies 51
Festival Commission for Cultural Development 95
Forces' Museum 49
forts 32,88
Four Paths 87
France 56,73,105,106,113
franchise 100,102,
Free village 60-62,64,93,98,99
French 55,56,59,75,89, 105,106114
French immigrants 25
full free 98
funeral(s) 3,9,19,118
- homes 30
- services 19
Garvey, Marcus 44,99,100
genealogical research 39
genealogy websites 51
General Register Office 38
generation(s) 1,4,18,36, 39,53,79
Georgian Society of Jamaica 50
German 55,56,57,59,73,75,77
- immigration 105,106,107
- indentures 57
- museum 49,57
Germany: place names
- Bremen 106
- Waldeck 106
- Westphalia 106
Ghana 59
Gibraltar (Europe) 89
Gleaner, The 36,44,86
- Archive and Library Service 45
Gordon, George William 99,100
government 20,21,23,87
- forms of in Jamaica 36,99,100,101-102
- housing schemes 22
- land 22,103
Governor 21,34,59,89, 97,101,106,111

Governor Eyre 99
Governor-General 33,34,85
- Achievement Awards 34
graduation lists 35
Grange Hill, Westmoreland x,86
grave(s)
- locations 26
- registrations 27
great houses 56
Great International Exhibition 72,94
Greek Orthodox Christians 72
Green Island 86
Guyana 67
Haiti 65,86,106,113
Haitian Revolution 65
handbook(s) 41-42
Hanover 15,30,98,106,*121*
Hanover Historical Society 49
Highgate, St Catherine x
Hindu 80,115
- temple 115
- tradition 82
historic sites 48
historical societies 38,49,50
Holland 105
Holland, St Elizabeth *68*
Honduras 109
Hong Kong 69,70,81
House of Commons (London) 97
House of Representatives 100
household
- extended 2,81
- nuclear 80
Human Employment and Resource Training (HEART) 96
hurricane(s) 84,112,113
illegitimate 79
immigrants 53,55,67,*68*, 69,70,72,78,80,81,104, 105,106,107,113
indentured workers 55,103
- Africans 63-65,67,108
- Chinese 69-70,108
- East Indians 67,108,115
- Germans 57
- Irish 55

Index

- Scottish 55
independent immigrants:
 - from India 67
 - from China 70
India 65,67,80,82,84,107,108
India: place names
 - Bombay 67
Indian 53,55,67,*68*
 - Immigration Law 107
 - marriage 80-81
 - music and culture 37
 - nationals 84
 - repatriates 110
Indians *see* East Indians
inheritance 20,82,103,104
inscriptions 29-31,32
Institute of Jamaica 34,41,42,49,75,94,95
international exhibition 72,94
International Genealogical Index (IGI) 27
Internet
 - sources / websites 37,40,45,47,50,51,52,71,123
inventories
 - properties 21
Ireland 73,105
Ireland - place names
 - Belfast 106
 - County Antrim 106
 - Ballymoney 106
Irish 55,56,58,75,77,89,106,107
Islam
 - African 63,66
 - Indian 115
Islamic (Muslim) 63
Island Records Office 27,38,47
Jamaica Advocate 43
Jamaica Agricultural Society (JAS) 99
Jamaica Archives and Records Department 38,40,45,47,78
Jamaica Baptist Union 25
Jamaica Battalion 90
Jamaica Broadcasting Company (JBC) later known as Radio Jamaica 87
Jamaica Broadcasting Corporation (JBC) 87

Jamaica College
 see Walton Free School
Jamaica Cultural Development Commission 95
Jamaica Defence Force (JDF) 32,91
 - records 32
 - website 123
Jamaica Gazette 33,34
Jamaica Herald 58,88
Jamaican Historical Review 71,72
Jamaica Historical Society 51
Jamaica Infantry Volunteers (JIV) 90
Jamaica Information Service (JIS) 45,47
Jamaica Inheritance Act, 1762 104
Jamaica Institute of Technology / College of Arts, Science and Technology (CAST) 95
Jamaica Labour Party 100
Jamaica Legion formerly Veterans' Association 32
Jamaica Library Service (JLS) 94
Jamaica Military Band 90
Jamaica Militia 31,32,33,88
Jamaica National Heritage Trust 38,48-49
Jamaica Progressive League 100
Jamaica Public Service 87
Jamaica Regiment 90
Jamaica Reserve Regiment 90
Jamaica Scholarship 94
Jamaica Territorial Regiment 90
Jamaica Tourist Board 45
Jamaica Union of Teachers (JUT) 94
Jamaica Workers and Tradesmen Union 100
Jamaica:
 - civil service awards 34
 - coins / currency 110-112
 - emigrants 104,109
 - funeral traditions 3
 - Independence 3,32,91,102

 - motto 53
 - population 36,72-74,104
 - proverbs 4
 - railway 86-87
 - surnames 77
Jamaican citizen(s) 2
Jamaican genealogy 52
Jamaican Military Service 32
JAMINTEL - Jamaica International Communications Ltd. 88
Jehovah's Witness 25
Jericho, Hanover 65
Jewish
 - cemeteries 30,57
 - Genealogical Society 51,57
 - Synagogue 57
 - tombstones 30
Jews 26,55,56,57,58,72,82,96,102,105
 - Brazil 105
 - Cayenne (French Guiana) 105
 - Curaçao 105
 - Czechoslovakia 107
 - Egypt 107
 - Germany 56,105
 - Poland 107
 - Austria 107
 - Guiana 105
 - Russia 107
 - Suriname 56,105
jobbing
 - job slaves 60
John Wolmer
 - Trust 92
Judaism 113,114
Justices of the Peace 35,42
Kingston x,30,36,43,56,*64*,67,70,75,80,82,86,87,92,93,94,99,100,111,112,114,115,*120,121*
Kroo Coast 108
Lacovia, St. Elizabeth 30,*64*,106
land
 - deeds 23,43
 - grants 22,40
 - ownership 22,47,103-104
 - settlement schemes 22
 - surveyors 22
Land Valuation Department 48
 - certificates 23

127

landowners 22,29,31,36, 57,60,77,102,104
Law 6 Registers 28
Laws of Jamaica 39,69
Lebanese 53,55,71-72, 74,77,107
Lebanon 71,109
Legal Aid Act 100
Leile 25,65,114
Lethe, Hanover 65
Letters of Guardianship 21
Liberia 59
library(ies) 36,45,47,75
- catalogues 37
- University of the West Indies 45
licences 19
Little Theatre Movement (LTM) 94
local government 101
- elections 102
logwood cutters 97,109
London Diocese 25
Love Lane, Kingston 94
Love, Robert 43,44
loyalists 65,89,106,114
Lyssons, St. Thomas 68,70
mail service 85-87
- sea 86
- air 87
Manchester 26,30,35,60, 62,63,94,98,99,*121*
Manchioneal, Portland 62,86
Mannings (High School) 92
manumission
- records 36,40,66,78
maps 17,24,29,41,43,48, 57,66
Maroons 55,63-64
- settlements (map) 64
- War 89,97
marriage(s) 6,19,20,26, 27,28,29,32,36,38,39, 40,72,76,78,80,81
- certificates 9,19,23, 24,39
- officers 26,27,81
Maternity Leave Law 82
matriarchal system 79
Matrimonial Causes Act 82
May Pen, Clarendon *x*
members of boards and

associations 42
- government boards 35
- government commissions 35
- Statutory Boards 35
memorials 29,30,36
merchants 36,44,55,56, 67,69,85,107
Metcalfe 60,108,*121*
Methodist 24,25,26,61, 78,93,114
Mexico 87,111
Mico
- Charity 91
- College 50,92
- Lady 91,92
- Museum 50
microfilm 27,43,45
Middlesex 31,106,*121*
migration
- patterns 83,84,104
military
- cemeteries 30,32
- records 31,32
militia 31,32,33,88, 89,90,97
Ministry of
- Agriculture 45
- Education 35
missionary(/ies) 24,55,58, 62,74,91,96,113,114
Mocho, St. James 68,75
money 39,49,62,72,83, 103,104,106,110,111
Montego Bay, St. James *x*,30,31,43,48,67,87,95, 98,106,115
Montego Bay Times, The 43
monumental inscriptions 18,29,30,31,32,
Morant Bay, St. Thomas *x*,30
- Rebellion 99,112
Moravian 24,25,26,63, 74,91,93,104,114
mortgage agreements 20
Mount Horeb, Hanover 99
municipal boards: originally vestries 102
Munro & Dickenson Trust 93
museums 36,38,49,57
- Hanover 49
- Bank of Jamaica 49
- Mico College 50
- People's Museum of

Craft and Technology 51
- Port Royal 51
- Seville Great House and Heritage Park 51
- Taino 51
- German 49
- Forces, The 49
Musgrave Medal 34
Muslim 63,80,82,115
Myersfield estate, Westmoreland 70
name(s)
- nick / pet 8
- maiden 39
- ethnic origins 74-77
- monuments 31
Nanny 97,100
Nanny Town, Portland *64*,97
national
- airline 88
- awards 33
- hero(oes) 100,112
- honours 33,34
National Archives 21,22,34
National Festival of Arts 95
National Housing Trust 104
National Library 24,33,35, 36,37,38,41,47,51,52, 95,116
National Workers Union 100
Native Baptist Church 55,114
naturalization papers 39
naturalized: citizenship 2
naval
- officers 31,32,55
- records 18,32
Negro Education Grant 93
Nevis 50,105
New Testament Church of God 25
Newcastle, St. Andrew 30
newspaper(s)
- back issues 36
- clippings 41,43
- titles 18,29,36,43-44, 45,112
Nicaragua 109
Niger 59
Nigeria *54*,59
non-conformists 28

Index

Norman Commission 104
Norman Manley 47,100
North Carolina 89
Northern Caribbean University (formerly West Indies Training College) 35,96
Northern News and Provincial 44
Nova Scotia, Canada 64,98
nuclear family 78
- households 2
nurses 95
Observer, The 29,88
official records 9
Old Harbour, St. Catherine *x*,25,86,87
Old Harbour Bay, St. Catherine *x*,67
oral history 8
Overseas Examination Office 35
overseas sources 18,52
Palestine 71
Panama 1,66,109,110
- canal 67,69,71,84, 109,110
- Darien 56,105
parent(s) 2,5,6,7,9,12,15, 29,42,69,79,91,92,93,96
parish(es) 24,26,31,40,47, 70,74,78,112
- capitals 23,30
- court houses 46,47
- homecomings 16
- maps 24,*120-121*
Parish Council: originally Parochial Board 29,35,102
parish registers 27,29,40,77
Parliament
- members 35
Parochial Board (changed to Parish Council) 102
Passage Fort, St. Catherine 85
patents 43
- of Land Grants 40
- boundaries of 43
paternity 82
People's Political Party 99
People's National Party 100

Philadelphia, St. Ann 64,99
Philippo, James Rev. 98,99
photographs 17,19,21,41,42,45,48,52, 116,118,119
pickney (field) gang 79
pimento 57
place names 24,74-75
Planning Institute of Jamaica 45
Plantain Garden River 65
plaques 19,28,29,30,32
Plum Pen, Hanover 65
Police 33,41
- Academy 33
- Administrative Branch 33
- Force 88,89,90
- headquarters 33
- promotions 33
- ranks 33,89
- records 41
political rights 57,89
Pond River Treaty 97
Port Antonio, Portland *x*,30,86,87
Port Maria, St. Mary *x*,30
Port Morant, St. Thomas *x*,56,105
Port Royal 30,51,85,112,*120*,*121*
Portland 26,30,62,70,75,92,93,9 7,106,107,113,*120*,*121*
Portuguese 30,55,59,107
Porus, Manchester *x*,62,*64*,87,99
post office 85-86
postal service 39,86-87
post-emancipation 44,60, 63,67,76,84,86,89,92, 98,104,107,109,115
powers of attorney 39
pre-emancipation 36,84, 85,88,91,92,96,103,106, 109,114
Prerogative Court of Canterbury (PCC) 21,27
Presbyterian 24,25,26,58, 61,*74*,93,99,104,114,115
primary school 16,91
- teachers 94
property tax 23
- receipts 22,23

property 20,21,62,80,96,99,101, 103-104,110,112-113
- titles 20,22,23
- slaves and children 79
Protector of Immigrants 80
public (government) secondary school 95
public office holders 18,34
Public Opinion 43
Public Record Office, Kew 21,32
public records 40
public servants 42
Quakers 27,62,93
radio
- programmes 37
- stations 87,88
railway 71,86-87
Rastafarian 115
Reggae Sunsplash 95
regiments 31,32,88-91
registered title 23
Registrar General's Department (RGD) 20-21,27,28,38,40,46, 47,52,58
registration centres
- district 9
religious denomination 60
representative government 102
Resident Magistrate Court 39,47
reunions:
- family 3,12-15
- school 16
- parish 16
right to vote / voting rights 96,99,101,102,103
Rio Bueno, Trelawney 61,*64*,106,115
riots 84,89,99,112
Roman Catholic 25,69,72, 93-94,102,113,114
Royal Gazettes 29,43
Royal Irish Constabulary 89
Royal Mail Steam Packet Company 86
Rusea's High School 92
Salvation Army 25,115
Sandy Bay, Hanover *x*,*64*,99
Santo Domingo 86

129

scholarships 35,94-95
school 16,20,65,91,93-96
 - elementary 93,94
 - attendance records 9
 - Free 91,92
 - high 16,84,92,93,94
 - magazines 35
 - secondary 16,35,42, 93,95
School of Art (the Edna Manley School of Visual and Performing Arts) 96
Schools' Library Service 95
Scots 55,56,105,107
Scottish 58
 - immigrants 105,107
Scotland 73,105,107
 - Culloden 105
 - Stranraer 107
Seaford Town (German) 56,106
self-government 100,101
Seventh Day Adventist 94
Sharpe, Sam 98,100
ship lists 23,36
ships
 - Epsom 108
 - S.S. William Pirrie 107
 - Theresa Jane 108
 - Vampire 108
shipping: Imperial Direct Line 87
Sierra Leone 61,64,65,98,107,108
 - workers from 65
Silver dollar 110-111
slave(s) 20,60
 - couples 80
 - women 20
 - families 76
 - households 79
 - lists 36,58,66,78
 - plots 43
 - revolts 84,106
 - runaway 63,97
 - trade 60,63,79,97-98, 105,106
 - uprisings 31,97
 - villages 79
Sligoville, St. Catherine 62,64,98
small farmers 22,99,109
small holdings 104
small pox 112
Society of Friends (Quakers) 56,62,93
Spanish 25,26,56,59,78, 85,88,101,103,110,114

- Crown 59
- immigrants 25,55
- immigration 105
- influenza 113
- Maroons 63
- names 74,75
Spanish Town, St. Catherine x,22,30,33,43,56,86,89, 92,98,101
sportsmen/women 94
St. Andrew('s) 26,30,60,70,92,120,121
St. Andrewe's 120
St. Andrew High School for Girls 93
St. Andrew Rifle Corp 90
St. Ann 16,26,92,56,61,62,92, 93,99,106,107,121
St. Anne's 26,120,121
St. Ann's Bay x,30
St. Catherine('s) 26,30,58,62,63,70,92,9 8,106,120,121
St. Catherine Free School 92
St. David('s) 26,120,121
St. Dorothy('s) 26,120,121
St. Elizabeth 16,26,30,56,62,93,98,10 5,106,107,114,120,121
St. George's College 93
St. George('s) 26,120,121
St. Helena 63,108
St. Hilda's Diocesan High School for Girls 93
St. Jago 85
St. Jago de la Vega 85
St. Jago de la Vega Gazette, The 43
St. Jago Gazette, The 43
St. Jago High (formerly Beckford and Smith) 92
St. James 26,30,61,92,97,98,106, 108,120,121
St. John('s) 26,58,60,120,121
St. Joseph's Teacher Training College 94
St. Katherine('s) 26,120
St. Kitts 56
St. Marie's 26,120
St. Mary 26,30,70,97,106,108,121

St. Thomas 16,30,56,65,99,105,108, 121
St. Thomas in the East 26,70,106,121
St. Thomas in the Vale 26,61,121
St. Thomas ye East 26,120
St. Thomas ye Vale 26,120
stamp(s) 86,87,110
state church 113-114,115
statutory board(s) 35,87
statues 29
step relations 2,9
street car service (trams) 87
Student Loan Fund 95
Supreme Court 21,39,46,47
Surinam 56,105
Surinam Quarters 56
surname 8,28,76,78
 - marriage records 27
 - child 8,76
 - countries of origin 77
 - death records 27
 - ethnicity 76,77
 - family names 8,76
 - father's 76
 - mother's 8,76
Surrey 31,121
Survey and Mapping Division 48
survey diagrams 20,22-23
Syria 71-72,107
Tacky 97
Taino 55,56,75,104
 - museum 51
tax 94,97
 - receipts 20,22-23
 - rolls 36
teacher training college(s) 91-92,94
telegraph system 86
telephone(s) 85,87,88
 - directories 24,36,46, 47,84
 - radio 87
television 87
The 19th Century & St. James Gazette 43
The Gleaner (at one time called *Daily Gleaner*) 29, 36,37,43,44,45,86,109
theological colleges 35,115
Titchfield Free 92

Index

titles: property 20,22
- registered 22,23
tombs / tombstones 82
- estate owners 29
- inscriptions 29,30,32
trade unions 99,100
traders 55,72
tramcar/trams 87
transport 85,86,87
Trelawny/Trelawney 26, 30,44,61,62,93,98,106, 115,*121*
Trelawny Town, St. James 64,97,98
tributes 19,28,118
Trinidad 67,108
trophies 19
Ulster Spring, St. James *64*,75
United Kingdom 21,33,56
United Kingdom and colonies 2
United States of America 3,44,57,65,67,70,86,87, 89,105,109,110,114,115
Universal Adult Suffrage 100,102
Universal Negro Improvement Association (UNIA) 99
university 16,35
- graduates 35
University Hospital of the West Indies 95
University of London 94
University of Technology (UTECH) formerly College of Arts, Science and Technology (CAST) 35
University of the West Indies 45,63
Up Park Camp 30,32,49,90
Vale Lionel (Porus), Manchester 62,*64*,99
Vere 26,108,*120*,*121*
Vere Free School 92
vestries 101,102
Veterans' Association (the Jamaica Legion) 32
Villa de la Vega (now Spanish Town) 101
voting rights 96,101
- franchise 100,102

Walton Free, later known as Jamaica High School, now Jamaica College 92
war volunteers 90,109
Ward, Charles 94
- Theatre 94
website addresses 40,45,47,52
wedding invitations 19
Welsh 55,74,75
West India Reference Library (WIRL) 41,94,95
West India Regiment 89,90,91
West Indian Federation 90
West Indies College (Northern Caribbean University (NCU)) 51,94,96
West Indies School of Nursing 95
West Indies Training College 35
Westmoreland 16,26,30, 56,57,91,92,97,98,105, 106,108,*120*
- Blue Castle 70
Westwood High School for Girls 93
widows 20,79
William Wilberforce 97
wills 20
- letters of administration (adoms) 21
- probated 21
wives 69,79,96
women 60,69,76,78, 79,81,82,90,94,102
- married 8,20,79
Wolmer's Free School 92
- Boys School 92
- Girls School 92,94
World War I 90,110
World War II 90
York Castle High School 93
Yoruba 59

131